MORECAMBE WINGS

MORECAMBE WINGS

The RAF and Morecambe (1940-1946)

Trevor Jordan 2014

MORECAMBE WINGS

Copyright © 2014 Trevor Jordan
All rights reserved.
ISBN-1499369832
ISBN-13: 9781499369830

MORECAMBE WINGS

DEDICATION

To Bob Crow 1961-2014 a giant among trade unionists his like we will never see again.

MORECAMBE WINGS

MORECAMBE WINGS

CONTENTS

	Acknowledgments	i
1	Introduction and background	1
2	Aims and Strategy	Pg 10
3	Sources and Methods	Pg 13
4	Interviews	Pg 19
5	Findings	Pg 101
6	Conclusion	Pg 112
7	Bibliography	Pg 116
8	Photographs	Pg 119
9	Documents	Pg 133
10	Kensington House Visitors Book	Pg 142

MORECAMBE WINGS

MORECAMBE WINGS

ACKNOWLEDGMENTS

Fred T, Betty F, Kathleen G, Pat F. Maud C, Mrs. K, James R, James Mac, Muriel D and Doris T.

MORECAMBE WINGS

MORECAMBE WINGS

1 INTRODUCTION AND BACKGROUND

During the Second World War the government took over a large number of the seaside resorts of the United Kingdom including Morecambe. This take over took place almost as soon as war had been declared. Civil Servants were relocated from Whitehall and the armed forces prepared the way for vast numbers of newly called up personnel.

Morecambe became blue the RAF could be seen everywhere. The takeover was total each apartment, guesthouse, hotel or house owner

BY TREVOR JORDAN

was compulsorily surveyed and billeted with a certain number of RAF personnel.

Morecambe lies on the coast about four miles west of the city of Lancaster, from which it is now linked municipally. It didn't exist prior to 1889 having grown up with the coming of the railways from the three coastal villages of Bare, Poulton-le-5ands, and Heysham.

It was always known as a cheap and cheerful seaside resort, popular with the urban working classes from Lancashire and Yorkshire. They came in their thousands during the Whit Wakes weeks and so many Yorkshire men came it was nicknamed Bradford by the sea.

It has several claims to fame, Potted brown shrimps, all through seaside lettered rock was invented here and in 1928 a local fairground owner Frank Ashworth invented Bingo. Its most famous son is comedian Eric Morecambe and its most famous daughter is Dame Thora Hird. Comedian Colin Crompton called it Costa Geriatrica "the place where people go to die but forgot why they went", in reflection of large numbers of retired people here (Bingham, 1990, Preface+ P272).

In the Second World War 'The Midland Hotel' (Photo 1, P120) became the RAF military

MORECAMBE WINGS

hospital, 'The Grosvenor Hotel' offices (Photo 2 P120) The Clarendon Hotel' became RAF headquarters (Photo 3, P121) and 'The Broadway Hotel' (Photo 4, P121) more offices all requisitioned at two days' notice..

During the London blitz of 1940-41 424 children and 232 mothers arrived at the Promenade station as evacuees. Morecambe only received three enemy attacks during the whole of the war. Number 10 Lauriston Avenue suffered a direct hit on 13th of March 1941, when an elderly couple Mr and Mrs Hewitt were blown from their beds into the middle of the road and killed. There were 26 bombs dropped on Heysham Golf Course on the 30th of July 1940 resulting in only the death of one cow (Bingham, 1990, PP238+239).

By the winter of 1943 the resident population had grown to 67,000 three times the peacetime figure. The influx consisted of mainly RAF but including 3,000 civil servants. They took over most of the east end hotels from The Broadway to The Grand (now demolished), for the purpose of the government financial services postal orders

BY TREVOR JORDAN

department. It became known as Whitehall by the sea (Bingham, 1990, P244).

The ground floor of the Alhambra music hall (Photo 5. P122) famous later as the set for 'The Entertainer' with Laurence Olivier as Archie Rice became an RAF depot (Bingham, 1990, P270). The newly opened Empire Floral Hall ballroom (1940) (Photo 6, P122) demolished 2004 and replaced with Aldi became a NAAFFI but with so many forces the demand for entertainment the war gave Morecambe an all year round season (Bingham (1990) PP244+245).

At the start of war RAF received 136,000 called up youngsters mostly aged 18 to 20 but extended to 23 by October and 27 by May 1940 (Calder, 1969, PP51+54). However the leadership of the RAF consisted of gentlemen volunteer weekend pilots. Fighter Command had only existed since July 1936 and the RAF was considered the junior service for politicians and military men alike. That would change after the Battle of Britain in 1940 (Haining, 1990, PP44-47).

By June 1944 the peak strength of the RAF stood at 1,185,833 with a total number of aircraft of 55,469. The principal problem was

MORECAMBE WINGS

the training of aircrew and the skilled men occupying 350 different trades. Training Command was divided to form separate branches to deal with flying and technical training. The latter was responsible for schools teaching everything from chaplaincy to bomb disposal, as well as supplying trained staff to deal with aircraft and their associated equipment.

As the planes became more complex, such as R.O. Mitchell's Spitfire, they required skilled technicians to repair and service them. The RAF before the war didn't have these sort of people but when a substantial number of aircraft were getting damaged during pilot training, salvage units were set up to repair anything that would in peacetime be scrapped (Chant, 1993, PP76+77).

Civil Servants forcibly removed to Morecambe demanded a weekly billeting fee of thirty shillings with free return rail travel to London once a month, better meals including dinner at night and almost non-existent single rooms (Bingham, 1990, P244).

BY TREVOR JORDAN

At the end of June, 1940 the government decreed that the east and south coasts from the Wash to Bexhill on sea were closed to holidaymakers. In August this was extended from Berwick-upon-Tweed to Lyme Regis on the Dorset coast (Walton (1978) P188). This meant apart from Brighton which was exempt that only the west coast could take visitors but in Morecambe posters demanded "Is your journey really necessary?" but Morecambe viewed its patriotic duty differently.

In the 1940 holiday guide it asserted "today holidays are a greater necessity than ever and we feel by continuing to cater for the health and pleasure of the nation we are fulfilling a duty of the greatest importance". In order to confuse Hitler a street plan was omitted and where hotels were already billeting these were stamped not available but over a 100 remained open (Bingham, 1990, P243).

Morecambe Solicitor John Knape had remonstrated with the Ministry of Works regarding the lack of compensation enjoyed by the requisitioned hotels. How were his clients to find the fees to keep their children in public schools; or other private boarding schools (Bingham, 1990, P244).

MORECAMBE WINGS

The Winter Gardens (Photo 7. P123) popular before he war for all in wrestling found itself host to the Halle Orchestra and the D'Oyly Carte Opera Company. 'Highbrow entertainment' was not the usual fayre offered to Morecambe visitors service or otherwise. The Royalty Theatre (now demolished) featured Thora Hird each week in a different role memories of wartime evacuee and Calder, 1969, PP372+373).

As regards other entertainment there were nine cinemas, two piers, the Tower Ballroom, and the Palace Music Hall all now closed and most demolished.

The RAF link provided unfortunately the murder of two Women. Aircraftman Rodger Williams murdered his girlfriend, local women Elizabeth Williams. WAAF Joyce Jagues was strangled on the beach by the Headway Hotel (Photo 8. P123) i n April 1946. Soldier Walton Clayton clearly insane pleaded guilty and was sentenced to death in under two and a half minutes, in the shortest capital trial ever. The Home Secretary Maxwell Fyffe refused to

BY TREVOR JORDAN

commute the sentence (Bingham, 1990 P250) . He was hanged at Walton later in 1946.

In 1939 many lodging houses operated under the apartments system. The guest brought the meat and the landlady cooked it providing vegetables and perhaps a sweet.

It remained a minority taste until the early 1950's but by 1939 the boarding house system where the landlady cooked a fixed menu at a fixed charge was becoming more popular.

With the bad press associated with the term boarding house, some establishments redefined themselves as private hotels. It would be sometime before the comic landlady popularized by Gracie Fields and later Peggy Mount passed into history (Walton, 1978, PP1-12).

The four establishments discussed in this project come into each of the three types. The Highfield (Photo 12, P125)and Victoria Street (Photo 10, P124) were apartments, The Kensington (Photo 11. P125) was a boarding house and The Ruperra (Photo 9, P124) (2001) and Photo 13, P126 (1943), was a private hotel.

In the Edwardian era it was habit to name guesthouse after origin of host. Ruperra in

MORECAMBE WINGS

Wales its miners would find a welcome there, perhaps where their own distinctive welsh accent was spoken or a local Welsh delicacy would be served. The habit of naming houses after the origin of the keeper was done to maximise business to attract persons from Ruperra and bring them back year after year (Walton, 1978, PP93+94).

2 AIMS AND STRATEGY

Very little corroborative primary or secondary evidence is available to evaluate the accuracy of the oral interviews. It was essential to develop a strategy so as to get as clear a picture as possible from the interviews made.
Detecting the difference between the anecdotal and the seemingly factual information to validate historical findings was essential, but there was an awful lot of gossip malicious and otherwise which has been discounted. Pages

have been omitted from interviews – where partners have elicited such discourse.

Allowing the interview partners free range with little supporting evidence from other sources this project is ideal to test the benefits and disadvantages of interviews as a means of presenting evidence.

The answers were ambiguous so then similar questions were asked to the subsequent partners who then provided information relevant to the next set of interviews. Then the original interview partners were contacted to get feedback from them as regarding questions not asked. Various questions were asked in the findings of a similar nature so the interview partners corroborated each other with the small amount of primary sources available. A rigid compression on the project question of RAF and their billeting arrangements with its effects on landladies, their experiences and the consequences for them after the war has been undertaken.

Two landladies were interviewed along with two children, one grocer, one housewife, and four service personnel (two RAF and two

BY TREVOR JORDAN

WAAFS) making ten interviews in all. The subject was so absorbing further interviews could easily have been taken but the maximum allowed was ten.

The logistics of having the population of Morecambe trebled every day of the year, turning it into effect a garrison town would not be without its problems. Were their differences between RAF and WAAFS being more demanding on their hosts. Did friendships become created or was their antipathy towards some or all of the guests.

A lot of the partners look fondly back to this period indeed many of them were children or young adults at the time. Their experiences seemed to leave an indelible mark on them and influenced their later lives. Was this the golden age myth or really was it a special time to them.

3. SOURCES AND METHODS

The wartime billeting records for Morecambe cannot yet be scrutinized. RAF records at Gloucester only covers the last ten years and the air historical branch at Bentley Priory since 1971. Prior to that they are held in the Public Record Office at Kew but will not be available for inspection until 2045.

The only other primary sources are contemporary newspaper cuttings and some editions of the RAF station magazine, Morecambe Wings, held in Morecambe local studies library. Wings does contain the memoirs of the senior airmen in the billet and the problems of officers on paying billets duty

BY TREVOR JORDAN

The Guesthouse visitor's book from the Kensington House has entries from RAF and WAAFS. With limited Primary sources available the only Secondary information on billeting is very small and omitted from most books of the period. General RAF background came from Spitfire Summer (1990) by Haining, the History of the RAF (1993) by Chant Showbiz Goes to War (1992) by Taylor with meagre information from Calder (1969).

The history of Morecambe is contained in one source 'LOST RESORT The Flow and Ebb of Morecambe' by Roger K. Bingham (1990). Information on seaside landladies comes from 'The Blackpool Landlady A social history' by John K. Walton.

'The voice of the Past by Paul Thompson has been used to together with A422 Offprints booklet to evaluate the problems associated with interviewing. Detailed background evidence not being available the interviews themselves provide the evidence evaluated methodically to separate fact from fiction.

To get as wide a view as possible the maximum ten interviews have been undertaken not just the four ladies involved in running the hotels and Guesthouses. A wartime Grocer, a wartime housewife with evacuees and then four ex-service personnel (two RAF and two WAAF5)

The Life History approach was followed starting with basic childhood questions leading to why the persons involved came to Morecambe during this period. From there the War was broached and interview partners encouraged to elicit a conversational approach where possible (Thompson, 1978, PP196-203).

The first interview with Fred T took on a rigid more formal controlled style of questioning (Thompson, 1978, P196). The reason being Fred needed more encouragement to elicit information than some of the others who once started were reluctant to stop. Fred did go on when relaxed to talk about wartime memories of El Ale main after he was called up but of no relevance to this project.

Two interviews took place with actual landladies themselves (Kathleen G and Maud C) so it is possible to see how the memories of the person in charge differs with those who helped mother after school (Betty F and Pat F).

BY TREVOR JORDAN

Kathleen G was a happy reminiscer (Thompson, 1978, P164) easily filling six hours of tape but she did own up that she did enjoy this period and met her husband through it. The memory process depends not only on comprehension but also on interest (Thompson, 1978, P113).

This sort of recollection singles out those moments that generated lasting experience before reconstruction took place (Niethammer, 1979, P72). Oral life stories can never be unmediated accounts but are dependent on how the brain stores memory. The remembered past is selected, omitted and distorted (Giles, 1992, P95). The memory process relies on perception through the basic process of ordering the human mind overcomes the problem of chronological memory. When the material is recovered the brain reconstructs it having discarded some memory it judges not to be important (Thompson, 1978, P111).

Niethammer (1979, P69) talks of "a fascinating account of his experience lasting more than two hours until he discovered that his cassette had run out after twenty five minutes". The second interview taken with Betty F was extremely interesting she was an

MORECAMBE WINGS

interested speaker talking a lot of useful data but the tape recorder's variable speed playback malfunctioned and the last hour was unintelligible.

The interview with Pat F showed the complex relationship between nostalgia and consciousness (Grele, 1991, P64). She reconstructed some of the past based on her later experiences as an air traffic controller and the award of her British Empire Medal in 1969. The correlation between wartime and post-war becomes merged she returns again and again to her post-war occupation.

"The threads of consciousness are difficult to unravel because past and present attitudes are so liable to be tangled up" (Samuel, 1976, P82). Almost every individual life breaks across the boundaries between home and work (Thompson, 1978, P257). "Story tellers are capable complex inventions and historical speculation about their testimony..." (Grele, 1991, P54).

The sixth interview that took place with Mrs. K was difficult she stamped her personality on the interview. She answered a

BY TREVOR JORDAN

question with her own question that it felt like the interviewer was actually the interviewee. Grele (1991, P54) had the forceful personalities of both Mel and Bella with both interviews simply question and answer sessions. What was excellent about this interview was she fitted into the hostile bigot that could be expected to occur in most random samples (Thompson, 1978, P123).

The four interviews with service personnel were illuminating to see what the feelings of them were towards their training and accommodation. Three in Morecambe for basic training only remembered the pleasant, unpleasant or humorous parts of their stay. The other interview with Games R an NCO RAF physical training instructor gives an insight into the training schedule, regime and discipline within the RAF regiment. Thompson (1978, P197) states "the more one knows, the more one is likely one is to elicit significant historical information from an interview". There was originally three times the information as most of the interviews took three hours each, though Kathleen G took six hours.

MORECAMBE WINGS

4. INTERVIEWS

Fred T., 19 June, 2001. Pages 20-24.
Betty F., 4 July, 2001. Pages 25-39.
Kathleen G., 9 June, 2001. Pages 40-60.
Pat F., 10 July, 2001. Pages 61-71.
Maud C., 10 July 2001. Pages 72-80.
Mrs. K., 17 July, 2001. Pages 81-86.
James R., 5 August, 2001. Pages 87-92.
James Mac., 4 August, 2001. Page 93-94.
Muriel D., 7 August, 2001. Pages 95-96.
Doris T., 11 August, 2001. Pages 97-100.

I wish to acknowledge the invaluable help given by the above interview partners.

BY TREVOR JORDAN

Fred T

TAJ: When war started what did it mean to you personally? I am not talking about later on when you did your war service.

FT: Well it meant it brought a great amount of trade to Morecambe with all these people being brought here for training you see. They were put into boarding houses. Everywhere in Morecambe had...every house in Morecambe had to take them you see these big houses, they were packed with...(Pause).

TAJ: Did people still come on holiday here?

FT: Well I think that, yes I think it would cease during the War I have really forgotten.

TAJ: The hotels were requisitioned.

FT: Yes the hotels were requisitioned you see (pause)

TAJ: Not just for hotel accommodation, but for office accommodation.

FT: Office and I think hospital maybe that sort of thing.

TAJ: Any idea, have you any memories of hotels being used for war purposes.

MORECAMBE WINGS

FT: I can't tell you which were used for what purpose no, no...(pause)
TAJ: We have these rather large hotels like The Grosvenor.
FT: Yes I only know they were taken over some by Officers and some for offices.
TAJ: When did that take place?
FT: Very quickly after the war.
TAJ: Late 1939.
FT: Yes I should say so...(Pause)
TAJ: Rationing didn't start straight away but you being in the Grocery business milk etc. how did rationing affect you?
FT: It was immediate once it started everything was rationed you see and became rationed and err if it wasn't rationed you only had a portion of this that and the other.
TAJ: How did the war affect the business?
FT: It brought a great amount of trade actually to Morecambe with all these men. Some of these boarding houses were I think for twenty. Sixteen to twenty, thirty men every day of the week and they had to be provided for. There were no supermarkets in those days. All the shopping was done round the shops. It was

BY TREVOR JORDAN

very hard work for the landladies to keeping the all these people happy, working to feed them. To look after them fully did a bed and brakefast that sort of thing. They lived in the house and that was it for how many months they were here, (pause)

TAJ: There is the other side of the coin the business improved. Was it seasonal or was it all the year round.

FT :It was all the year round during the war yes of course.

TAJ :It came after the war the seaside landladies would have had a worse business really.

FT: No after the war it increased because there were so many people wanting to come away on holiday that hadn't been able to take holidays. There were still no motorcars for the ordinary person you perhaps realise so they all came here by train. Train loads of them to Morecambe from all the Cotton towns of Lancashire and Yorkshire so Tykes (Yorkshire men). Ah yes and there was terrific business for many years and then of course people began to go abroad and they found the sunshine and it began to trail off ...(pause). There was very good trade for many years in fact there were so many

MORECAMBE WINGS

people came on holiday that to Morecambe that and I say there were no motorcars they couldn't walk on the pavements in Albert Road at meal times everyone went onto the beach, onto the promenade after brakefast and they all came back to a mid-day meal that sort of thing and the streets were full and you couldn't walk on the pavements you walked in the road. There were so many people (laughs). Every house was full choca-block with them.

TAJ :How was it affected on the ration, how did it affect the meals?

FT :How many guests the boarding house took they claimed for so many people you see and they were registered for so many people and they had maybe only ten in one week or twenty in the next but they claimed groceries for ten people or twenty people you see as the case may be.

TAJ: You any memories of the ration you being a Grocer?

FT: We had to snip this was immediately after the war you see and now rationing came about during the war I am not certain of when. We

BY TREVOR JORDAN

had to cut out from their ration books tea, butter, sugar all the rest of it was all listed.

TAJ: Was the food in greater supply.

FT: Well I think I said in Morecambe we were very lucky there was plenty of food as so many people had to be provided for during the war and then after the war of course we had all these people coming holiday so it was kept up.

TAJ: Do you remember anything about the seaside then with the soldiers here?

FT: Only that they trained in the streets every street was full of soldiers, marching up and down near the Alhambra then which is on the seafront yes. Coughs.

TAJ: Do you remember how Wartime affected the attractions, music halls etc.?

FT: The theatres were all of course full, some of the finest actors and actresses in the country all came here to The Winter Gardens or the Tower. Some of the finest shows as well everyone of any note at that time came here to Morecambe. The Winter Gardens was one of the highlights of the country at that time. The place was packed with thousands of troops every night of the week.

MORECAMBE WINGS

Betty F

TAJ: Did you have any choice whether you became billets?

Betty F: No we asked that and we couldn't it was taken over. They came round and inspected it and told us how many we could take. You couldn't have two in a bed they all had to have a separate bed so we had 14. Started off with 14 RAF and later on we had WAAF's but not together of course.

TAJ: So you had either male or female.

Betty F: Yes, yes we started out with the RAF came for their foot slogging along the Promenade for six to eight weeks. They had all their injections at the Midland Hotel which was the hospital and then they went to their different stations to be trained for whatever they were going in for and later on we had

BY TREVOR JORDAN

them for sixteen weeks training as riggers and MT drivers. Mother ran business with my Father helping until he was asked to go into the Intelligence Corp inspecting boats from Southern Ireland. They carried on with this business until the war came. But my Mother ran it herself I helped her I was training as a Dancer at the time and err I did my practice after I had helped my Mother during the day. We had an Auntie who came to clean the bedrooms but we did expect the RAF to wash up at teatime, that was the only thing we expected them to do and they didn't mind at all. We were allowed 1.0/6d a week for each person for a full breakfast. They weren't in during the day they were out and they came back at teatime. You had to provide them with a hot meal then but Mother also made cocoa and biscuits at night. A lot didn't go out at night because they were tired but weekends were the time they went out. There were a lot of cinemas in Morecambe eight or nine and three live shows, two piers and they were full every night. There weren't many visitors as the hotels had been taken over. The Clarendon, The Grosvenor was taken over by Civil Servants from London, The Elms Hotel, The places on

MORECAMBE WINGS

the Promenade, The Broadway or The Headway they were all taken over. At Heysham we had the army tank corps as well. It was mostly RAF, mostly blue that you saw on the Promenade.
TAJ: When did they start to come?
Betty F: 1940. War was declared in 1939, September they started coming just after Christmas.
TAJ: When did they go?
Betty F: oh right until 1943. My Mother finished up with for a week some for just a night or two nights coming back from abroad. Some were injured and going to hospital in Manchester. We did have some that stopped with us 18 months they were having treatment in hospital.
TAJ: Was it 1947 before you saw the last of them.
BF: No it was 46 because I opened it as a dancing studio then.
TAJ: So did it cease to be a Guest house.
BF: Yes my Mother never had it as a Guest house again because I took it over.

BY TREVOR JORDAN

TAJ: Seaside landladies were better off in the war because after the war they only had seasonal business.

BF: Yes that's true but soon after the war a lot of landladies took in workers who came to the ICI and that sort of thing. Instead of having guests to come and stop urn they took over these working people. A lot of RAF did stop in Morecambe after the War... We did have two bedrooms we kept for wives that came over at weekends or for a week holiday because I had a bedroom of my own and my sister had her own bedroom and she went into the forces. So we had a spare bedroom which my Mother used if someone came to stop, husbands or parents ... but she was full of RAF until after the war.

TAJ: So there were no visitors other than with the forces.

BF: We had one big room tables at one end and sitting room was at the other where you sat so you couldn't split them up from the RAF or guests. We had no fridge in those days everything was kept in the cellar on cool slabs.

TAJ: What problems did you have with rationing?

BF: When you had 14 in it isn't like having a family of 4 because you have 2 ounces of butter

MORECAMBE WINGS

with 2 ounces of sugar. When you think of 14 together you can make something with all that you got we never seemed to run short of food in our house and then we had an Auntie who came from the country Shropshire, she to bring eggs, chickens, rabbits and that sort of thing and then we had the rations of meat we used to queue up for: slices of beef.
TAJ: Did RAF get a ration book.
BF: No you didn't you had chits off them, they came round to pay you on a Monday morning. The warrant officer came and paid you and they gave you chits to give to the butchers shop or grocers shop. He knew you had for 14 so you had 14 two ounces of sugar etc.
TAJ: Would they get a mid-day meal the days they were off?
BF: No they went to the NAAFFI or they had sandwiches. A lot just had a good breakfast and then they had a meal when they came in the evening.
TAJ: Where was the NAAFI?
BF: I think there was one at the Savoy Cafe, a lot went to the Clarendon and there was the Arcadian Theatre on the Promenade and The

BY TREVOR JORDAN

Empire. There was an Empire Cinema, Empire cafe, Arcadian restaurant and the Arcadian cinema so those were used as well... They did have shows I trained a team of WAAF dancers to entertain the forces at St. Laurence's church RAF club in the evening. The Odeon on special days had top stars coming to entertain the RAF personnel alone no civilians.

TAD: Did you remember any?

BF: Yes there was George Formby, Gracie Fields, they were the top ones until Gracie fields married an enemy alien when she was not well thought of during the war. We had some famous people are our house: Simon Eden Anthony Eden's son and he went out to Burma from our house and he was killed out there. We had a lot of letters for him, my Mother sent them to Anthony Eden and she got a lovely letter back. Sarah Churchill came, Winston Churchill's daughterwith the warrant officer on a Monday morning to pay us. Freddie Mills the boxer was a PE Instructor. It was a jolly time during the war there was plenty of entertainment. We got all the London shows at the Winter Gardens, The Halle Orchestra came and the ballet companies came. I knew Eric Morecambe and Thora Hird because I had my

MORECAMBE WINGS

first dancing lessons off Thora Hird she couldn't afford to furnish her front room and she had tap dancing lessons on Saturday morning. I went to school with Eric, I used to dance with him at the Mickey Mouse club on a Saturday morning. Eric Bartholomew in Euston Road school and we used to do shows at night his father used to be a whistler, famous tunes he used to whistle them. He used to go round all the talent shows and either Eric came first or his mother, his father, Roly Woodhouse played the drums, Peter Gambell used to sing and I used to dance.

TAJ: You were 12 at the start of war.

BF: Yes I was at school though' I left quite early and carried on with my dancing and helped my mother at the same time. I could practice soon as the airman had gone and weeks even after her husband went abroad and then she open a hairdressers in Morecambe...

TAJ: Where did the RAF do their training?

BF: The RAF were over on Westgate like an aerodrome there were hangers no planes and that was occupied for quite a while afterwards.

BY TREVOR JORDAN

When I opened my dancing school there was the odd RAF here even then.

TAJ: Was this the regiment rather than the pilot?

BF: Pilots came as well they still had to do their footslogging even if they were air cadets. They got their basic training and inoculations.

TAJ: was there any complaints with drilling in the street?

BF: There was no complaints that way. Some didn't treat the boys right I mean some didn't feed them as they should have done but there weren't a lot of those really. They were generally good to them really. My mother always used to say if my father was in the forces and my sister hoped someone was looking after them as good as she was doing. We encouraged them to have hobbies. We had the cellar we let them use it as a hobby place, we had singsongs around the piano, take them to church. Every fortnight we either went to Methodist or Church of England. We took them on picnics, took them on cycle rides all sorts of things. We did have aircrew coming back from abroad, Labrador and the Seychelles. I was only a young girl I stitched their stripes on, polished their buttons, and they used to give me a bar of

MORECAMBE WINGS

chocolate from the NAFFI it was worth it you see. It was a happy time in Morecambe. Eric Morecambe went to an audition in London during the war and stopped there, he did ask me to go with him. Later he was a Bevin boy but he had to stop that as his heart wasn't so good. He went to ENSA because my sister saw him in Cambridge in the war. he came to see me shortly before he died and we had a talk for a couple of hours.

TAJ: If you came from Morecambe and you wentin the RAF did you get your training here?

BF: Some did one was billeted with us but he never slept at our house but got a compassionate sleeping out pass. He went home to Regent Park, Blakey they had the toy shop next to the Clarendon Hotel and he was billeted at our house.

TAJ: Any problem with the ration?

BF: We had no problem with food my mother cooked huge rice puddings. When you get all the rations you can do a lot with it. She used to bake and make pies. I used to go queue up and then I started to teach dancing during the war. I taught ballroom dancing, tap and ballet. Quite a

BY TREVOR JORDAN

lot of Polish soldiers came... We had Gladys Hay, Will Hay's the comedians sister billeted with us. We used to have the wives come and stop with us, one lady came every weekend while her husband was here but when she was bombed she stopped with my mother for 14 slices of brawn, never see brawn in the shops these days. It used to look horrible in those days a bit like dog food. They were well behaved really.

TAJ: There was no trouble?

BF: The RAF military police didn't have a lot of trouble with them in our house a couple of times they came in drunk but they had to be in on time. It used to be half past ten. We never had much trouble. We used to have a bath rota with one bathroom and one toilet. Family had a toilet outside we had a rota for two baths a night but WAAFS wanted more. They wanted to wash their hair and they were more that way. They kept the bedrooms tidy but my auntie came to clean them, the officers came round and inspected just when they wanted

TAJ: Like they would have done in the barracks.

BF: they were told when they came in they had to respect the home. She kept her tablecloths

MORECAMBE WINGS

and carpets down but in the end she had to take them up they got threadbare and you never got paid for replacing anything like that. A lot didn't bother they took them up and soon as the RAF came in but my mother didn't. And she had to have linoleum on the tables where you could wipe down, like a tablecloth made of linoleum. It was rubberised and had patterns on, fruit patterns. You see them when you go abroad on these cafes. She was sorry she couldn't use tablecloths but it was the washing we didn't have washing machines then. We sent it to the laundry or we did it downstairs in the basement.
TAJ: Did you get access to the forces laundry?
BF: No we had to do it ourselves.
TAJ: What about the coal ration.
BF: We had a fire in the kitchen and a fire in the front room for the boys. We seemed to get plenty of coal, that was put down at the front of the house. They used to take the lid off the coal cellar and put it down there. A lot used to live in the basement but we never aid. We had one room where we put all the cold food in, a big room where there was a drain. We used to

BY TREVOR JORDAN

do all the washing in there and the coal came in at the end there, we always had a fire in the kitchen as she cooked with ovens at either side of the fire. It was an American grate you had to black lead to polish it and you cooked like an American range. On first day I got scalded that's why I took dancing lessons as my legs weren't straight.

TAJ: You had no trouble with WAAFS wanting to go out every night.

BF: We never had any trouble like that. We had a Belgian air gunner called Teddy who took a giant teddy bear to the cinema and bought a seat for his teddy. Aircrew used to do things like that and I know he was very keen on classical music. He used to put my record player on wind it up in the middle of the night, four and five o'clock in the morning. My father used to go up the wall and he was there for quite a while. He asked my father to borrow £10 he had to go to St. Johns Wood in London and we never saw him again.

TAJ: He never got his ten quid back.

BF: It was a lot of money in those days. We didn't have a lot of trouble only the odd drunk. I used to teach dancing in Queen Street where there was seven pubs and I hated drunken men.

MORECAMBE WINGS

So when I was teaching dancing there my mother used to send somebody to meet me and bring me home and this is the actual one who came to the reunion. He was with us for eighteen months he was like a brother to me and used to meet me so I didn't have to come up Queen Street on my own. It was a street where there was a lot of trouble, but it wasn't always the RAF it was civilians, and forces home on leave. When Army came from Heysham and RAF were on the promenade they used to call them Brylcream boys. I have been asked here.about the Midland hotel but it was a military hospital and we didn't go there it was a restricted area. We only got one bomb up at Heysham on Lauriston Avenue demolished one of the houses but no-one was killed. I never heard it I believe one was dropped in the bay going towards Barrow you see. People were injured but no-one was killed. We never went out without as gasmask it was the fashion to have lovely colours on the case. I went to Euston Road School and we had air raid practices but we never had an air raid. We were lucky here you wouldn't have thought the war

BY TREVOR JORDAN

was on but for the uniforms. Where there were boarding houses with five or six bedrooms it wasn't worth having the RAF they used to house evacuees. A lot came when their fathers were in the forces it being the seaside and stayed here. The home guard used to be down Victoria Street by the visitor office and I used to be a runner taking messages from one home guard unit to another, practicing if we were invaded. We all had stirrup pumps in the house to put out the incendiary bombs but we never got any of those in Morecambe but only person we saw was warrant officer on Monday paying for billet. We provided sheets and pillowcases but RAF provided blankets and beds but we got paid no extra for washing.

TAJ: When I interviewed Fred he said there was plenty of food.

BF: There was, we never got bananas unless you were a child ill with colitis. We never got oranges at all and we never saw bananas until after the war. With relatives in farming at Christmas auntie came with turkey off the ration. Some just had boiled eggs for Christmas day did some of the lads. I had a lady's WAAF ballroom team and we made the dresses out of

MORECAMBE WINGS

blackout material and scrimp. That was worst part you had no light anywhere.

TAJ: I take it your Mother never had any rest 365 days a year for 6 years.

BF: She never grumbled even if she was awaked in the middle of the night. Auntie used to relieve if my mother wanted to go away for the weekend but she had to coincide it when my father was on leave. It was a happy time for me I made friends and I am still in contact with some of them. Thora Hird lived down Cheapside quite near us.

TAJ: Thank you for your time

BY TREVOR JORDAN
Kathleen G

KG:: In those days the style was for persons to bring their own food.

TAJ:: Used to call that Apartment boarding house.

KG:: That's right but we decided that we would make it into a private hotel and we would take full board. I can't remember if whether it was 7/6 or 8/6 for the full week but my Mother was a very good cook because her mother she had been a cook for Lady Beaumont at Beaumont Hall. My mother was brought up to be a better cook and I was a baker and confectioner so we were able to make quite a bit of lolly out of it because doing that you can make more profit doing everything for yourself which we did. Anyhow we had a full twelve months absolutely fully booked and then the war broke out and we were fully booked then until October. When the war broke out we only had one man turn up on the Saturday morning. The rest had paid up and gone out Friday night and we got all ready for the Saturday influx and nobody turned up but this one man. They were coming round with loud speakers telling all the holiday makers to clear out, they wouldn't

MORECAMBE WINGS

guarantee to get them home even. So they had to go home immediately but this was out on the wireless and of course people didn't come. Anyhow that was that it was quite a shock because when we came in we never thought about war breaking out, never entered our heads. We were so busy we carried on and we were doing quite well. After that they came round to see if we would take civil servants but they said that you could get 21 shillings a week but they had to have separate rooms and wardrobes and dressing tables and it wouldn't run to it. You couldn't make any profit so we turned it down and then a few weeks after that they came round again and said we had to billet. In the meantime we got holidaymakers kept drifting staying a week at a time, anybody who dared risk it. We used to take em in (coughs) then (pause) came round and said we had to start billeting. We will take four and take a few visitors as well. Oh no you can't you have got to billet, you can't take visitors and so.
TAJ: It was compulsory.
KG: It was compulsory you had no choice and so we said we would have 8 but anyhow when

BY TREVOR JORDAN

we reckoned it up it was 19/6 a week and you had to give them two meals a day. It didn't matter about supper but we did. You had to provide breakfast at 7.30 am (Parade was 8am) and a tea and after that you weren't supposed to give them anything but we always brewed up tea for anybody that came in and gave them a snack of some sort even if only tread and jam. There again with being able to bake and do everything ourselves it made a big difference. They supplied us with folding beds so we decided to make some money out of it we would take a lot more, not even try and sneak visitors in which we kept trying to do and we decided to take the extra. It gradually grew we went up to 12 and then about 20 because the pressure was on to take more. We decided...

TAJ: You could only put one in a bed.

KG: They were supplied with blankets which they took in every so often to fumigate but we had to supply sheets. I cut the sheets we had and I cut them into singles and made pillow cases and contrived to give them two pillows each. So they had two blankets and to keep warm they used to put their overcoats as well over the beds. Winter it was very cold. My two little girls we went onto the beach which we

MORECAMBE WINGS

weren't supposed to do and we got big boulders and carried them downstairs we had a great big kitchen and there was an old iron fireplace as big as the back wall. It was flat on the top and two ovens at the side. We had a little annex at the back where we had two gas ovens. We didn't use these ordinary coal ovens we bought coke because it was cheaper but we had pans that could go all along the top. These ovens at the side we put these boulders in and could take at least half a dozen in each of the ovens and sometimes 8 and wrap them in a piece of flannel and we gave them one each to put in the bed. But they had to bring them down in the morning to go in the oven again and we said if you don't bring your boulder down you don't get one. They all religiously brought their boulders down and so that's how we kept them warm in the winter. I don't suppose everyone was as soft as we were. When they came at first they were only boys, they were only about 18, youngest they could take was 18. Some of them the first lot came from Wales, some had come off the farms and never seen a toilet, a water toilet. They had been used to outside closets

BY TREVOR JORDAN

and they were so young it was really sad. We used to have them for three to four weeks. When they went at first mother and I used to shed tears as they were all applying to be aircrew and we wondered if any ever got back but then you get hard to it you are not so soft. As time went by they got older and older and we had all varieties. They would march them from the railway station in Lancaster then pair off so many for there, so many for here all along the road. Then go down the next street and do the same. You never knew who you were getting all shapes and sizes. We never had any trouble it was hard work, they were all male though WAAFS did come later. We had quite a few WAAFS in for a short time but it was harder work with the WAAFS because you had to supply so much hot water. The men weren't as much bother as the women. It used to be quite a problem with these women and some of them were ladies and yet they hadn't a clue. They were supposed to do the potatoes and things like that. My dad he always used to peel the potatoes but my dad used to show them how to but in the finish we had to get a potato thing that you turned with a handle because they were more bother than what they

MORECAMBE WINGS

were worth. It used to be hilarious my dad trying to show these girls because they hadn't a clue. All they knew how to do was have their baths and tart themselves up and wash their undies. There used to be underwear everywhere and with the sanitary towels they used to keep putting them down the toilets. We would have the toilets blocked up so every time when we got a new batch in we had to tell them to wrap them in newspaper and bring them down and we would put them into the fire. The times we had to get a plumber to keep the toilets clean and every night the boiler was going full tilt for hot baths, they were really hard work and we had to get the iron and board out but you had all that to supply and so it was easier continuing with the RAF.
TAJ: How long did you billet for?
KG: We were billeting right up to the last three or four months of the war. Sometimes you would get what you were supposed to get but they would come round asking you to take more because a lot had got killed and they were wanting more men. Downstairs we had the dining room it was a big room, table down

BY TREVOR JORDAN

there and then in the kitchen we had a long table. My mother and I would stand behind and there were two men detailed from the dining room to come and fetch the dinner plates. After that there was puddings.

TAJ: How did you feed 20 in a house this size.

KG: It was easy 11 rooms and in the big rooms and in the attic you could take 4 and in room above you could take 4 and you could take 4 in here and 4 in the next room. Then there is a room where I sleep now a big bedroom well there is one above there and we could put 4 in there all in these single beds and in every room there was a wash basin which made things easier but we had only one bath and we had to have a rota but we had two toilets. For our personal use we had a toilet out in the backyard. We were lucky with having a billet the supplies were brought into the town. I used to be in with Tomlinson's butchers in Albert Road he couldn't go into the forces because he had a bad heart. He wanted to join up very badly but he was a nice young man but they wouldn't take him. He used to be very good Tony he used to get me 7 pound tins of corned beef and I used to make corned beef pies flat pies with onions and thick gravy, potatoes and

MORECAMBE WINGS

vegetables. There was an allotment down over by the school, we were able to get plenty of vegetables when the shops hadn't got the supply. Tony used to save me beast hearts cow hearts we used to boil those overnight and we used to make stuffing and apple sauce and we used to call it mock goose but the lads used to love it but they didn't know what they were eating. They said what lovely meat they wouldn't eat it if they knew what it was. We used to get quite a lot of eggs and great big tins of jam, plum and apple. We had dried eggs of course, tins of SPAM and tins of milk. We were short on fats but we could get margarine and we were fortunate. My dad's friend worked at the Town Hall and he used to deal with the tea coupon and we used to get tea from away and anyhow he was very good he used to let u have extra tea coupons. We weren't t allowed but we got extra tea from town hall. So we could always make plenty of tea with bread and I used to make scones, cakes and buns and things of that sort. The flour used to be pretty rough but when I couldn't buy the bread I used to try and make it. Same with teacakes and I used to make

BY TREVOR JORDAN

puddings as well. They used to go mad about puddings the lads because some came from down south and they thought it was marvellous how we could bake and cook as we did. It was really a wonderful time it's no use saying I didn't enjoy it because I did I enjoyed every minute of it and that's a shocking thing to say but it's true.

TAJ: You didn't have them that long.

KG: We had them for three weeks but sometimes we had a professor and her was tall he was six foot something and I don't know what size of shoe he was. They couldn't send him on as they had no boots for him and we had him for a week or two until they could get him fixed up. This was when it was the older ones that came. When the blitz was on we had in the middle of the night the red caps knocked us up and brought a young woman Grace and her husband was billeted with us came from Slough there was a big shelter and it took a direct hit. She was absolutely distraught and it upset her so much because they were all killed in this blitz. She got on the train and came up here and landed at Morecambe station where the redcaps picked her up. We used to have a little room where my two daughters slept and I

MORECAMBE WINGS

slept next to them but if any wives turned up like that or sometimes they asked if their wives could come for the weekend they used to bring my two girls into my bed and let them have this little room. We weren't supposed to but we did as we liked. The poor thing was with us for weeks and weeks but her husband was not a bit pleased to see her. I could have smacked him instead of being sympathetic he thought she should have stopped where she was. He wanted us to refuse to have her and send her back but in no way was I going to send her back the poor thing. We weren't supposed to keep her but we did and she was with us quite a while before she could pick up courage. I think until the bombing ceased up.
TAJ: There wasn't any here
KG: they used to come over and be after Barrow and there used to be a mock aerodrome at Silverdale. They used to bomb Silverdale. further along they dropped two bombs and it was two old people who got killed in Fairfield Road going up towards Heysham way and it got a direct on the house and they said they were just jettisoning the bombs were the Germans

BY TREVOR JORDAN

because of the anti-aircraft. The shrapnel used to rattle on the roofs but that was the anti-aircraft that was going on. The roof at the back there all the tiles were broken from the shrapnel but no one was hit. We used to go to the Whitehall cinema once or twice when we've been there in an air raid and it used to scatter on the roof when you were watching the picture with my two little girls with me. It was hard going because when they were transferred they didn't all go together, they would call one or two outside by six o'clock. Then other didn't have to go until eight, the rest of them. The day they were all going we always used to put a proper breakfast on for them having saved the bacon ration and an egg and sausage and porridge. We used to fry spam and make fritters and dried scrambled egg on toast and jam. You can make dried egg quite tasty. With dried eggs I could make some lovely sponges. Fish we could get plenty of which we fried and we could get smoked haddock. He used to come with a barrow but the round got so big he bought the fishmongers at the top of Regent Road. A lot of the fish, small cod and haddock came from the bay but they used to make a good meal dipped in batter, fritters a boiled egg

MORECAMBE WINGS

or a fried egg. No restriction on jam and bread and you could get salads, sliced onions and boiled onions and liver. We all used to go dancing there was the winter gardens and the central pier, the old tower there was dancing every night. Lads used to go they used to meet different girls from round and about. We used to have a clocking in board, they had to be in for ten o'clock but of course they never were and we never used to try and enforce it. I mean they were grown men if they are old enough to fight they're men. When they came in they'd peg in and when all the pegs were in we would lock the front door but they got crafty and if anyone wanted to come in late they opened bottom window downstairs. We never let them know we knew what they were doing. One aircraftman asked could his wife come but then anyone with a single room would vacate so the wife could share. The wives weren't supposed to eat with the fellas they used to come and eat in the kitchen. We had all settled down for the night when all of a sudden there was such a scream going on it was terrible we got up, my mum and dad got up and the lads they all got

BY TREVOR JORDAN

up. Everybody was on the landing. There was screaming coming from the top room. One of the lads had walked a girl home to Overton and it was in the middle of the night when he got back. He couldn't get in and what he did was climb up the fall pipe and climbed through the window. Well this wife saw this figure coming through the window. She yelled frightened everybody to death. We settled everybody down it was really hilarious. I said to this lad why didn't you ring and he said he had a right job dodging the redcaps getting home and I didn't want to make any noise and I thought I could get in there. The fall pipe was rotten and you could see the foot marks where he had walked up the wall. He had to go on parade then next morning just the same. When it was inoculation Saturday they never used to get anything to eat. You would be surprised how grown men are frightened of needles.

TAJ: That was in the Midland Hotel

KG: Some of them were terrified, they used to come and some got so poorly from the injections they used to get and they were confined to billets. That weekend we were so busy. You were supposed to leave them to their own devices but you never did we weren't that

MORECAMBE WINGS

sort of people. One lad fell down in the passage outside here. My bedroom door it was shut there and he was such a big fellow he filled the door. He had collapsed you see. I had to stand on him to open the bedroom door so we could see to him that way to fetch him round. My poor mother some of them used to have this yellow fever it used to be awful they used to be really ill and one time there was one he was desperate in the night. His pal knocked my mother up and we got on the phone to see if the MO would come and he said he would get there as soon as he could but he was very busy. This man was so feverish she said I will have to sponge him down with cold water he is so ill. I said I'll help you but she said "oh no you can't" but I had two little girls it tickled me did that but there again that's how we were at the beginning of the war. He was dreadfully ill and the MO didn't come until 9 o'clock the following day and praised my mother as she had saved his life. My second husband I met him while he was billeted with us and I fell for him hook, line and sinker anyhow he was transferred abroad and he was away three years

BY TREVOR JORDAN

and then we got married. When he returned we had stopped billeting we had gone back to Private hotel then. There was another funny incident the billet emptied out and they said we wouldn't be getting anyone in. One lad and he had to go to the hospital came back unexpected after we had re-enamelled the bath. We

used to leave the doors open then. He got in the bath and stuck to it requiring to go back in the hospital to have the enamel removed from his bottom (laughs). Then they used to go church parade they were supposed to have their dinner at twelve o clock straight after church parade. A lot of the used to go to Park hotel for a drink so I said to my Mother we would alter dinner to one o clock. We used a gong to summon them across the road, if you don't come immediately you won't get any dinner. It worked but Johnny Knape he is a solicitor, he was, he retired long ago. He was an officious bloke he really was, he came round and said he'd heard we had altered the dinner times. I said it was better the men could go have a drink he said they shouldn't drink. I said that's beside the point they do. He said it's against the rules. I said this is our house and that's that we make the rules here not the RAF. He said we would

MORECAMBE WINGS

hear further but we never heard anything. He was narrow minded treating them like schoolboys and I know we had an artist from Australia Johnny Wood he used to draw some beautiful pictures. He did two for every wall all ladies transparent you could see their figures through, nothing lewd fully dressed. He came looking round the dining room and checking everything was alright checking the billet and he said they'11 have to come down. I said whatever for he said it wasn't seemly among men puts ideas into their heads. We had a right to, about that they are not coming down. This was Johnny Knape he was right high up in RAF he was too old to fight but he was one of the big boys. He was a solicitor he came back to soliciting (laughs) oh that sounds awful. Jobling and Knape I think it was called. All the rules and regulations the> had it was quite ridiculous. Expected them to give their lives and treating them like schoolboys. With the redcaps you never saw any real bother only every now and then when soldiers came to the camp. We had two sexual murders, two WAAFS that were murdered. One was married to Barbara who

BY TREVOR JORDAN

lived on here two doors down and she was married to this soldier. She was in the WAAFS and she met him while she was in the WAAF and he had been overseas. She used to come over on leave and anyhow he got this WAAF and he murdered her strangled her on the beach down the other end by the Headway hotel on the sands there. They found out who it was and came and arrested him and he was hung. Another airman he came off the caravan site and he stabbed and killed a WAAF so we had two murders. I think he was hung but they certainly hung the Then we had a corporal cocky cockney who demanded a single room. I refused but he turfed out the occupant showing his stripe. I retorted I made the rules but after his reply I put a complaint in and had him transferred.

TAJ: Did you have the right to remove them?

KG: Oh yes any bother you could put a complaint in if they were a nuisance or they didn't comply they were out. We didn't have any real bother only this cockney and a group of WAAFS. We had this Manager of a big cinema but he was big and fat but he couldn't do his training and was discharged. We had a retarded girl Polly who used to clean the

MORECAMBE WINGS

bedrooms and he was demanding breakfast in bed. I went and told him off but I felt real sorry for him he couldn't manage to do the drill, he used to come in exhausted. I got into trouble with my Mother with the toilets one group couldn't hit the toilet and it used to be swimming. Only this particular group I told them if they couldn't hit the pan I would get them a perch to stand on the mucky so and so's. Everyone broke out laughing my mother said how could you say that. I used to get chased by those wanting extra pudding but I told them they had to agree between themselves who got the extra. The younger ones were timid but the older ones used to corner me and tickle me I used to be awful ticklish. The times people told me they loved me but one I felt rather sad. The RAF welfare came an airman being rehabilitated had got badly burnt and we were told to look in their face irrespective of what revulsion you felt as if he is normal. He really was bad all scarred and disfigured but he was so nice he had been a stockbroker. He gave me a letter saying he loved me, he couldn't kiss me but he kissed me with his eyes. That really moved me the nicest thing anyone had ever said to me. When my future husband came back I burnt the letter. It was a sad time and a happy time. When they went away they used to buy us drink, flowers and collections. Not a lot but they would have a collection. With the canteen the children used to get chocolate and sweets RAF always used to bring things. When we got teachers they used to teach art and music and literature rather than go dancing. So I could go out dancing at the Winter Gardens or the Central Pier the older men used to look after the children. It all worked very well.

TAJ: Do you remember anything about your dealings with billeting authorities?

KG: We did start out with 19/6 but with some chivvying we got it up and I was appointed to act a spokesman for all the billets on this road because they said I had the gift of the gab. I used to stick up to them I used to go to the headquarters and see Flight Lt Hughes who was nice.

TAJ: Where was that?

KG: The Clarendon hotel on the promenade. They said we had to get ready for a big push coming in and we all bought in for extra billets

MORECAMBE WINGS

coming in. They never turned up and we had all this food and when they came at end of week to pay you there was no pay, they weren't going to pay us. I was delegated to go down and on the front by the Clarendon a photographer said smile and snapped me but I snapped back. A Flight Lieutenant name I have forgotten saw me, he was later done for bigamy. He married a Morecambe girl but they found he was married twice resulting in a famous court martial. They said it wasn't their fault. I said of course it was their fault we wouldn't have bought in if we had known but they conceded it and we got our money. I have a snap of that photograph on the promenade he was very brave (shows it) In finish we got 21/- which rw.de the difference giving us profit which we needed. We still had our overheads you didn't get a reduction in your rates, no reductions on anything. You had to buy in there was no such thing as Sunday trading and we kept food in the cellar which was pretty cold but we had to use more or less immediately. When one batch went away in the morning another arrived in the evening so all day you would be changing beds as we always

BY TREVOR JORDAN

put clean sheets on. Shows pictures of house, you see I was Preston and My mother and father were Sheppard. They came and took the iron railings but they left the metal form it was too bulky to go on the lorry.
TAJ: What did you call the Hotel.
KG: Ruperra that was the name on it when we bought it in 1938, the name of a welsh mining village, this is the ole Whitehall cinema with my two little girls, this is an old horse called Ben which we kept on fields behind.
TAJ: Profit from hotel bought a horse.
KG: We had to sell it because it was too old.
TAJ: When did you leave the hotel trade.
KG: After the war we did it for a year or too up until 1952 but when I married my husband my mother and dad got too old.
TAJ: Thank you very much

MORECAMBE WINGS

Pat F

TAJ: Did your mother have help in the Guesthouse?
Pat F: She had myself and my sister when we weren't at school. She had kitchen help. I remember an Evelyn Howes as she was called up to the WAAF and married one of the airman that was billeted with us.
TAJ: How did you become a billet?
Pat F: They just marched up and told you how many airman you got and we had 15 from day one. Others locked their doors and went away but we had no chance.
TAJ: You weren't obviously allowed to keep guests at the same time?
Pat F: Well we had one room with a spare bed in it and the billeting authorities told my mother she could take two evacuees but she said don't you think I've got enough to do I have two young daughters, I have 15 airmen and two doctors coming for lunch every day.
TAJ: Some guesthouses kept a spare bed for the wives or families of the airmen.

BY TREVOR JORDAN

Pat F: Talking off the record everyone had to have their own bed whether it was a double or a single. When any of the wives came to visit the men would double up but it wasn't really allowed. We had weddings we lived very well we had all the extra rations. My mother had to go to the town hall every week and quote how many cups of tea she had served and how many meals she had served and then she had to go up to the Savoy cafe where she got paid a £1.0.5d a man and if he was away that was reduced. They only came with blankets we came from north Staffordshire, the potteries and with being in the catering business with hotels we had quite a considerable number of china tea service, dinner service my mother used all that. She used all her own sheets, she was one of 14 and she had five sisters and a brother in the army and she thought if someone was looking after them she could look after somebody else's. The testament to all that is in here (produces visitors book). She was very good, very clever we lived very well but she had to do all this. It wasn't considered work of national importance because she also had to do fire watching at night. Every girl she had to help her was called up, I was called up at 17.

MORECAMBE WINGS

TAJ: You say your mother had to collect her money other landladies said the warrant officer came out to them.

Pat F: It's all vague but I do remember her going to collect her money and rations. There was no coal ration for these men or women. The hot water had to come out of our coal ration but you did get the rations. The Savoy cafe on the Promenade next to the Royal Hotel is where they paid out. This book is full of testimonials, a lot of the service people who were stationed with us.

TAJ: The first entry RAF 25th of April, 1940. Did you ever see any of them after the war.

Pat F: We kept in touch with Stan Skidmore until he died last year. There's a lot in there then we had the WAAFs.

TAJ: Do you have any special memories of the WAAFs.

Pat F: Yes the first group I can remember them all. We had three different lotsof WAAFS. The first group undertaking basic training and then we had a second group who were office workers and they had been sent up to Morecambe and one or two of them were wives

BY TREVOR JORDAN

of officers from the various forces and the third group were the nurses from the Midland Hotel that was the hospital. The middle group my mother had laid the table in the big dining room, the fire was burning and the girls didn't sit down to their meal. My mother suspected something was wrong and shortly afterwards there was a ring of the doorbell and several RAF officers stood there. Her first words were I know why you have come. You knew we were coming. My mother said no idea at all but I know why you are here and apparently these girls had put in complaints that they couldn't have hot baths every day, they could only have one every week and various other complaints. There was no coal ration for the service people so to heat the water had to come out of ours. The officer said they wished they were billeted with my mother because is this a normal meal. My mother said yes and they said we don't get as good as this. So they asked what shall we do with them. My mother said I'll tell you what to do split them up you are going to have to take them out I am not keeping them put the ring leader somewhere on her own as she will cause trouble wherever she goes. So they did and those WAAFS had to report every day and

MORECAMBE WINGS

every evening to headquarters and that was the only trouble we ever had. We had some very interesting people we had one man a black man a Nigerian who thought he was a cut above the rest until they tamed him. He called my mother his mother and my sister and I his two sisters. After the war we heard he had married several wives and was one of the richest men in Nigeria. He wanted to take an English girl back to Africa. Michael Savage was his name I have a photograph of him somewhere. We had then from Scotland, Ireland, Wales, the Hebrides, made a lot of friends and lived very well.
TAJ: Was the business better in wartime or before the war? Pat F: It wasn't a boarding house it had been bought by a wealthy grocer and he had built Kensington House and the row of houses. We were the second occupants of that house and he moved into one of the big houses on Morecambe road. My parents bought it off him and it came complete with servants quarters on the top floor and very big cellars. It was a massive big house and come 1945 my mother was in hospital and the services wouldn't take the RAF out. The doctor

BY TREVOR JORDAN

said she had to get out this house you are in now with me I have lived in this house since June 1945. It was the only house available for sale and I got the girls from the Ops room to help us move in.

TAJ: I take it keeping a billet made your mother ill?

Pat F: five and a half years she did it and I saw her crawl upstairs on her hands and knees. When we had people in transit she used to crawl out of bed in early hours of the morning to get their breakfasts. Eventually we billeted the permanent staff so there were less of those coming and going at peculiar times. A lot of people did the bare necessities but my mother succeeded in making it a good billet.

TAJ: Was there lino everywhere including the table tops?

Pat F: Carpets everywhere but there was no wall to wall carpeting then. I can remember the three piece suite in the sitting room went to the floor because you couldn't replace things. When we moved out we still had the airman in we walked out with what we could carry but we had to sell the house as it stood with most of the furniture in. We wouldn't have fit it in this place. The man who bought the property from

MORECAMBE WINGS

us next year he evicted the airmen and sold the building for double what he paid us. It was the only way we could get out.
TAJ: How many bedrooms did Kensington House have?
Pat F: There were 8 bedrooms.
TAJ: So the airmen had to double up.
Pat F: Yes two to a room but they each had a bed. We slept in the cellar but it was a beautiful house with stained glass and window seats on each of the staircases.
TAJ: The cellars were normally used to store perishable goods there being no fridges in those days.
Pat F: There were racks and racks of stored with apples and fruit of every kind so my mother could make something sweet out of it. She utilised everything she never threw anything away and there was a coal cellar in the middle and the other big cellar was the washing cellar. We had a massive great big kitchen with a great black range and that's where we had all our meals and then two big reception rooms.
TAJ: How long was it in operation as a boarding house before the war?

BY TREVOR JORDAN

Pat F: About two years but prior to us living there it wasn't. (Gets out visitors book). This is the Haymarket hotel Manchester (laughs). Shows later entries 1936 is when we came here.

TAJ: Some seaside hotels attracted clientele from their previous location. Did any from Manchester come here?

Pat F: Could have done but it was more commercial travellers than tourists there. It was near Free Trade Hall and got a lot of theatrical people. We were also a brass band family my father's lifelong friend was Harry Mortimer, very famous in brass band world. We used to get all the bandsmen even after we came to Morecambe. My father played the cornet and we were very involved quite a lot came to stay with us. After we moved here my mother carried on bed and breakfast but it was just a few guests not 15 airmen. They still had to live but with having to sell Kensington House at a loss they had to start again in a lot of ways. Everybody did it next door we carried on until 1949. By then I had a job and I was contributing and my father was on the Ribble (Bus company). I was an Air Traffic Controller for 30 odd years.

MORECAMBE WINGS

TAJ: Obviously taking one or two wouldn't generate as much revenue than 13 airman.

Pat F: What at £1.0.6d a man, not much is it but I think she'd had enough. My father suffered from first world war he was badly injured in his back he was chesty, he wasn't a fit man but he lived until he was 84 in 1980. My mother died in 1987 at 88.

TAJ: Do you remember anything from wartime other than the black Nigerian?

Pat F: My mother was very clever at making things out of nothing stretching the ration. When the boys got food packages from home they brought it to my mother. She was feeding them so well they didn't need it. My mother was classed as no two billet number one was on Skipton Street. (Looking at visitors book) I remember these WAAFS they used to give me collars as I used to wear a RAF uniform in the Observer Corps as we part of Fighter Command. I got more shirts than I was entitled to.

TAJ: There was never any romance with the airmen.

BY TREVOR JORDAN

Pat F: I was allowed to go dancing but I was too young. Every billet had a leading airmen who watched over the behaviour of the others. (Takes out group picture of WAAFS on Promenade in 1942).

TAJ: Can you remember any in the photograph.

Pat F: Those girls are mentioned in the visitors book at least ten of them were billeted with us. Second left at the top is Dorothy Griffiths always known as Griff. Second left bottom Rhoda Henderson and Peggy Short is second row at the end right hand side.

TAJ: A lot of the landladies didn't like the WAAFS as they didn't have domestic skills of use.

Pat F: That bunch in the visitors book were ok as were the nurses but the administration staff we had trouble with. My mother wouldn't let me go into the WAAFS having seen the behaviour of some of them. I don't know how true it was but faced with billeting some landlords gave the RAF the house. In handing it over the RAF became responsible for putting it right when the war was all over. What happened to us was wear and tear but you weren't compensated. There were stories that airmen were put out in the street and officers I

MORECAMBE WINGS

believe had to pay for their billet. At Christmas my mother said bring your friends round as some didn't get any different for Christmas. There were cases of boiled eggs being served for Christmas lunch but we had two or three times RAF who we should have had. A lot of the billets had tried to put guests in with the airmen. It made you think as they came here to be fitted out for service abroad and with the rumours troop ships had been sunk. They did send them somewhere else after leaving Morecambe and then changed the plans to save lives. The fifth column must have been there somewhere even in a garrison town. Some refused to turned into billets forcing the RAF to requisition their building but in so doing you handed to the RAF responsibility for damage and they had to return the building to its pre-war standard when they vacated. They also had to look after the men themselves but very few people did that most thought it was their patriotic duty to care for the RAF.

BY TREVOR JORDAN

Maud C

TAJ: How many bedrooms did you have?
Maud C: eight.
TAJ: What was it like running a business with your sister.
Maud C: Ok we always got on.
TAJ: on what basis did you run your business was it apartments or a private hotel?
Maud C: Apartments the guests brought their own food but if they wanted board we did that as well but not as a major part of the business, It was apartments mainly.
TAJ: When wartime came you had to provide board.
Maud C: When war broke out it brought us the RAF giving us no choice.
TAJ: How many did the billeting officer allocate to you?
Maud C: twelve.
TAJ: You weren't overcrowded.
Maud C: no they always had a bed each. Some of the bedrooms had two beds in so there was two in there. We had to provide them with food, give them their breakfast, dinner and

evening meal each day which they didn't provide us much for. I think it was a £1.0.4d a man.

TAJ: Did you have to collect the fee from the Savoy Cafe.

Maud C: No they brought it round depending on how many we had in that week. First we had the recruits, then we had WAAFs and we had permanent staff. The Girls then we had permanent staff with the lads, RAF.

TAJ: Those that worked in the Clarendon Hotel.

Maud C: Yes we had. No they were permanent PT Instructors, NCO's we had two warrant officers.

TAJ: Can you remember the meals you made or any problems with the rationing?

Maud C: My sister did most of the cooking we did our best with what we had, the money we had. I will tell you one strange thing. At Christmas some didn't go home but we got extra rations being civilians but the RAF didn't. I wrote to Food Minister Lord Woolton and asked him why servicemen in billets weren't allowed the extra rations because we wanted to

BY TREVOR JORDAN

make as good a Christmas as we can for them. Anyway we got it yes we did they just paid up and didn't argue.

TAJ: Did you have any problems with the RAF or the WAAFS.

Maud C: None at all. we got on really well with all of them we really did. We had some nice letters from the lads after they had left but I often wish I had kept some of the letters. How we had been so kind to them and helped them. It was first time they had ever been away from home.

TAJ: Did you have any problems with so many people in house at one time.

Maud C: There was no problems It was a big double fronted house and we had six cellars underneath and we had one with a great big stone table and that was the keeping cellar where we kept perishables. One was a coal cellar because we had coal in those days, back one was the washing cellar with a big boiler and sink.

TAJ: With coal on the ration was it difficult heating.

Maud C: Yes it was they were very big rooms it was a

MORECAMBE WINGS

difficult problem heating. It was a big cold house and hard work keeping it warm especially when it was freezing. There were plenty of blankets, plenty of bedding it was fitted up for the visitors. Normally there was only one in a bed but with apartment house there was two in a bed if you understand what I mean.
TAJ: Yes there were some quite lurid stories of seven in a bed. There were stories of landladies charging for the cruet.
Maud C: Good gracious me no oh heck nothing like that.
TAJ: Gracie Fields poked fun at seaside landladies.
Maud C: Yes that tale there was a joke about charging for the cruet when a couple leaving he was taking cruet with him and she asked what are you doing. Well he said I've paid for it I am taking it home with me.
TAJ: You couldn't mix troops with visitors though the odd wife turned up.
Maud C: Occasionally yes not very often only once I can remember. An RAF was in a room by himself so we told him it was ok.

BY TREVOR JORDAN

TAJ: Did the business do better before the war or during it as you ceased the business afterwards?

Maud C: Before the war it was much better oh yes when you had a house full of visitors they were paying a lot more than RAF even with apartments and you didn't have to provide their food. A £1.0.4d a week but you had to make it do, do what you could. We had 24 before the war four to a room two adults two children. We charged for vegetables or a sweet if they wanted it. There was no cooking at teatime they sorted their own tea out.

TAJ: You couldn't refuse to have the RAF.

Maud C: No not if you had the accommodation and we did have. Nowadays they wouldn't attempt to put a house full of men with two single women and we didn't think a thing about it.

TAJ: Some have said WAAFS weren't a lot of use you could get men to do chores but not women.

Maud C: No they were all alright I remember one batch of WAAFS we had and there was one girl a very nice girl a very quiet and I asked her why she wouldn't mix. It turned out she couldn't read or write and she was so ashamed.

MORECAMBE WINGS

The others helped her it was surprising what you came across.
TAJ: You being single you didn't get any attention from the boys.
Maud C: No
TAJ: You remember any incidents or some staying out late. Maud C: We had a rota
Maud C: Yes that tale there was a joke about charging for the cruet when a couple leaving he was taking cruet with him and she asked what are you doing. Well he said I've paid for it I am taking it home with me.
TAJ: You couldn't mix troops with visitors though the odd wife turned up.
Maud C: Occasionally yes not very often only once I can remember. An RAF was in a room by himself so we told him it was ok.
TAJ: Did the business do better before the war or during it as you ceased the business afterwards?
Maud C: Before the war it was much better oh yes when you had a house full of visitors they were paying a lot more than RAF even with apartments and you didn't have to provide their food. A £1.0.4d a week but you had to make it

BY TREVOR JORDAN

do, do what you could. We had 24 before the war four to a room two adults two children. We charged for vegetables or a sweet if they wanted it. There was no cooking at teatime they sorted their own tea out.

TAJ: You couldn't refuse to have the RAF.

Maud C: No not if you had the accommodation and we did have. Nowadays they wouldn't attempt to put a house full of men. At one in morning we locked the door but one night I was locked out. I remember someone coming and asking for a Cedric but we knew him as Bill when he had called up he dropped his real name.

TAJ: You remember any problems shopping?

Maud C: We were registered with the co-op in Regent Road it was a lovely shop and we got our bread from a little shop along Clarendon road. We had no problems with food. The more you had the better ration you got it was better having 12 rather than 8. We used to make Cheese dreams it was a cheese sandwich which we dropped in hot fat only meal I remember.

TAJ: You were never called up?

MORECAMBE WINGS

Maud C: I suppose we would have done if we didn't have the billet but I was a reserved occupation. I did have to go and register but it was as good as being in ATS or Land Army.
TAJ: Do you remember what the RAF did.
Maud C: They did plenty of marching on the promenade. A few garages were requisitioned and RAF did the vehicle repairs to teach them a trade when they went abroad. My husband when he first came to Morecambe was instructing with the RAF. I met him out dancing. I remember there being loads of entertainment. The floral hall, the winter Gardens, I have had some good times there. Picture halls there was Whitehall, Arcadians, The Empire, Plaza, Morecambe was a great place for entertainment during the war. The central pier, Tower ballroom oh yes the RAF and Officers very socialising place. Every night plenty of people. Flanagan and Allan came to the Winter Gardens, they brought some London shows, military bands.
TAJ: Did the billeting authorities inspect you?
Maud C: No you only had that if the troops complained but we had no complaints we even

BY TREVOR JORDAN
invited WAAFS to our wedding. (see photo 21 p132 for a library picture of such a wedding).

MORECAMBE WINGS

Mrs K

Mrs K: When we came here my mother in law wanted to move away from the Blitz. We swopped our bungalow for this house as you couldn't sell houses in wartime. We then took two further evacuees so we then didn't have to billet the RAF though all of our neighbours did.
TAJ: Were you assessed to take RAF?
Mrs K: Yes but I told them we couldn't do them as we had these evacuees and you couldn't do both.
TAG: Where were your evacuees from?
Mrs K: London and they were twins 8 when they came and 11 when they went. Mags they were called. Couple of little devils they were in a way I was glad when their mother came for them because they were untruthful and I couldn't abide untruthful people. Then the mother came for a holiday and she was horrible I didn't like her at all pushed herself in. I hadn't room for her really but she said she could sleep with the girls sort of very insistent.
TAJ: How did you deal with meals I suppose she had her own ration book?

BY TREVOR JORDAN

Mrs K: She said she would have the children's fair share with the children. She didn't go without Morecambe did very well for rations with the RAF being here. There were no shortages of food whatsoever even in those families who didn't have RAF. You had friends and farmers we went short of nothing. We didn't do anything illegal but we didn't go short or have anything under the counter.

TAJ: Did you do any war work.

Mrs K: I had the family my son, the evacuees so I looked after the house fire watching in a building around the back here which is flats now.

TAJ: Apart from one bomb there wasn't anything else was there?

Mrs K: No there was more in the first world war when they blew up the ammunition works. We had no troubles here. It was a very busy place during the war a very profitable place.

TAJ: Did you have any dealings with the RAF.

Mrs K: no not really we were friendly with them. They used to parade out here right along this road because there was a big garage at the end. My little lad who was 4 at the time I made him a little uniform and he marched with them as a little mascot. Long after the war he joined

MORECAMBE WINGS

the RAF. They were a busy lot and there was plenty of them and it kept the town going.
TAJ: The hotels were requisitioned.
Mrs K:. The hotels were requisitioned for the Highers up and the troops were in the boarding houses.
TAJ: With the RAF being here you had a 365 day season in the music halls and theatres.
Mrs K: Its terrible now when you think we had the Tower ballroom, then the Central Pier, then the Winter Gardens, then later on there was the Empire buildings with the ballroom, the Floral Hall. Hoare banks from Bradford built and they called it Hoare banks folly. There was the Palladium, the Plaza, the Odeon, the Whitehall, the Alhambra and the Palace and there is nothing now.
TAJ: how did you get paid for your evacuees?
Mrs K: I don't remember I don't think we got paid, I don't think we got anything for them. I think you just had them thrust upon you. Well you volunteered to have them. I don't remember getting anything for them. You got rations but you didn't get an allowance. I was a good baker all homemade stuff.

BY TREVOR JORDAN

TAJ: Did you get asked to billet others like civil servants.

Mrs K: They didn't come to common boarding houses. Though they did very well out of the RAF. They made a lot of money Easter to October you made your living and the rest of your time was your own. In war they had them all year first time any of them had to really work. They didn't have a hard life boarding house keepers.

TAJ: Some preferred peacetime as they said they made more money.

Mrs K:. Granted they didn't have to work 7 days a week but even so in the season were full Easter or Whit to October and rest of time you could rest. They wanted the money but not the work.

TAJ: The landladies complained the billeting fee was insufficient to cover wear and tear.

Mrs K: They make you sick, they wanted the money but they didn't want to do anything for it. I have dealt with them I know what they are like. Terrible people a lot of these boarding house keepers.

TAJ: Your evacuees do you remember anything.

MORECAMBE WINGS

Mrs K: Their mother was a nasty piece and I made them dresses but she was sort of woman you couldn't please. I think she had a good time while they were away. They had to pay towards their clothes and keep so she decided rather than pay she would take them away. Iris and Doris Maggs. it was a boom town during the war. It wasn't a busy rowdy town it was nice and peaceful. People made a living and they were honest with a lot of good shops which there aren't now.

TAJ: What about Johnny Knape the wartime RAF billeting officer?

Mrs K: Well the other one was called Robinson but I didn't like him.

TAJ: Is he the one found guilty of bigamy.

Mrs K: Yes but he thought he had an eye for the ladies but I didn't like him, he was a horrible .

TAJ: Any complaints about the RAF

Mrs K: No we kept ourselves to ourselves. Still do but we used to get letters from RAF who adopted my son as a mascot. Morecambe did alright out of the RAF no one can complain at all. A lot of guesthouses and hotels had been

BY TREVOR JORDAN

empty before the war and the RAF made the numbers up. They got round the year income they did better than a four month season. If they had been good landladies the RAF came back for holidays in peacetime with their families.

MORECAMBE WINGS

James R

TAJ: How did you come to be in the RAF ?
James R: I volunteered in 1937 before the war. I went to Uxbridge and came to Morecambe just after war was declared in 1940 and went to Blackpool in 1942.
TAJ: What did you do.
James R. Physical Training Instructor.
TAJ: Do you remember the billeting officers Knape and Robinson.
James R: The billeting officer was Warrant Officer Jones. John Knape was chairman of Morecambe football club.
TAJ: You were a sergeant in the RAF.
James R: Yes
TAJ: Where did they billet you?
James R: Mrs Scott, 103 Alexandra Road, we were there from March to August 1940. It was good one of the best. We were all NCO's in that billet about six of us. If we wanted to go dancing we went dancing we didn't have to be in by ten o'clock. They were 98% good landladies, some better than others, never had any trouble. If there was they would be on a

BY TREVOR JORDAN

charge and they knew that. We had to inspect the billets every day we had 10 or 12 billets a flight 144 men. The average was about 6 to 10 in a house. One or two of the bigger ones ten or twelve but that was about it.

TAJ: They got two meals a day.

James R: No they got three meals a day breakfast, dinner and tea. Some landladies even gave them supper. That was the extra good ones. One of the best ones we had was no 12 Marine Road she fed them well.

TAJ: I spoke to Kathleen G she married an airman billeted with her.

James R: That happened a lot, I got married here in 1940. There was plenty of good thing going on in Morecambe in the war. There were eight cinemas and two live shows.

TAJ: You didn't get the RAF and the WAAFS together.

James R: No the RAF went and the WAAFS come. There were still some RAF riggers here down White Lund.

TAJ: You did the PT on the promenade

James R: We did some on theside streets wherever you happened to be. Foot drill and rifle shooting down the White Lund rifle range.

MORECAMBE WINGS

Self-defence bayonet fighting was up at the army camp at Middleton Towers Holiday camp.
TAJ: One lady said they marched them off the trains at Lancaster.
James R: Not that I knew they always came into Morecambe. A troop train left Morecambe at 5 o clock every morning well we had to have the men there by then, it eventually went to London.
TAJ: You marched them down the Promenade.
James R: Yes we marched them down the Promenade. They did their passing out on the bandstand by the Midland hotel.
TAJ: Midland Hotel that was the hospital where they went for their inoculations, some became quite ill.
James R: Yes they would have done some probably got malaria, lot of them were quite ill those that got vaccinated. Those never vaccinated before came out in a big lump and were off sick for two to three days.
TAJ: Did they all come for basic training here.
James R: Yes they did their basic training here for three Weeks and then they went onto different stations for courses. They did physical

BY TREVOR JORDAN

training, self-defence and how to shoot a rifle or use a bayonet if they had to. It was only to get them used to discipline because they were all technicians. You had three months before the war to make up your mind which trade you wanted to do so I went for a physical training course. Before the war basic training was three months but during the war this was cut to three weeks After the war this was increased to six weeks. During the war you had more of them but you didn't have time to give them three months training. Above was happy with three weeks as they were all clerks, technicians or tradesmen but they were wasting their time. There was always problems there was no discharges if you didn't get through first basic training you did it again. We found some couldn't read or write but they were taught in the RAF. It was funny however bad they were they could speak English or count money. They were mainly Welsh who lived up in the hills and probably never went to school and probably their parents were the same.

TAJ: You enjoyed your time in the RAF?

James R: I would say yes

TAJ: Can you take me through the training day.

MORECAMBE WINGS

James R: They had a break once an hour doing different things starting at 8 o'clock with drill and PT and in the afternoon they went to lectures or down on the range. We sometimes went on the beach for PT.
TAJ: How did airmen numbers in Morecambe differ from other seaside towns.
James R. : Blackpool was the largest with 45,000 at one time. You got one or two deserters but discipline in the RAF was pretty lax offenders who stayed home after leave would get 14 days cv. The odd one went to Aldershot to the military prison. They were fair about it the RAF. Father's refused leave at time of the birth were treated alright. If you didn't have a pass military police were sure to pick you up. They would check one or two at random. There were six instructors in each flight one instructor to 24 men and police would ask them which flight they were in and to name their instructor.
TAJ: Did any one complain about the square bashing,

BY TREVOR JORDAN

James R: They were wasting their time complaints went into the headquarters and only misbehaviour was taken seriously.

TAJ: Any complaints about billets.

James R: The only one I had to deal with was where they didn't get enough food. He used to give them a slice of bread and butter and a slice of fat. He was told and it improved but it never became a good billet. We only had the one really bad one but we used to tell them to do what they would at home and don't break anything. Do as the landlady said if it was reasonable. I know they didn't get very much in form of recompense.

MORECAMBE WINGS

<u>James Mac</u>

TAJ: When did you get sent to Morecambe?
James Mac: I can remember coming to the seaside for my square bashing. I was short sighted so I was no use for aircrew but I decided to become a mechanic. It was to make us fit but most of us being 18, 19 years of age we were already reasonably fit. We did square bashing on the front every time we had a moment. They made you drill left right left right, turn right, turn left about turn this sort of carry on. We got route marches, cross country runs but it was a farce discipline was reasonably alright in the RAF. Obviously it didn't need to be so severe as it was in the army because being fitters and mechanics and that you couldn't order a man to do a job he had to be trained to do a particular thing and then get on with it. If he is a fighting man he has to have very severe discipline tell the man to go over the top and get killed. They had to know they had to obey but nevertheless it was laughable we were marched a few miles out in the country at a leisurely pace. We were then marched back but

BY TREVOR JORDAN

we only broke out into quick march as we passed the headquarters on the front. Then we eased off back to the pace we had before but discipline was not too harsh.

MORECAMBE WINGS

Muriel D

TAJ: When did you come to Morecambe.
Muriel D: In the WAAF in 1942. We went to Bridgnorth for a uniform and came back here for the square bashing as we called it. With Morecambe being so close to Cockermouth where I was born my mother came to see me march in the hottest summer ever which was very embarrassing. I was billeted on Westminster Road going towards Alexandra Road. She was not so good a landlady she didn't like the WAAFS and there were five of us to a bedroom 25 altogether. She was very strict I was five minutes late back to the billet and she locked me out. I had to sleep in a garage and she reported me for that and for hiding food. She provided these huge meals that I couldn't eat and I hid the excess in a cupboard which she found. I didn't get any punishment being put on a charge or anything. From the Central pier we used to march up to Heysham and they wouldn't let us take our jackets off in the really hot summer because above wouldn't give permission. We were

BY TREVOR JORDAN

absolutely roasting. I remember going to Burton's buildings for inoculations.

TAJ: Any other memories of Morecambe.

Muriel D: I went to the Winter Gardens to see Swan Lake being performed by the Royal Ballet.

TAJ: Any other WAAF memories-

Muriel D: I remember being terrified of the inoculations but I worried myself so much I came out in a rash. As it happened I was the only one in my section not to get ill but while the others were ill I had no-one to go out with. Burton's buildings was the corner of Euston road. I remember we had three meals in the billets she did feed us well I will tell you that. I didn't enjoy Morecambe I had blisters on my feet as you had to wear heavy shoes. I had blisters throughout my heels but there was nothing to do there were no RAF here apart from officers and they were too old. I was a volunteer and I had a sash to indicate this on my uniform. I was in a reserved occupation making pencils in Cumberland and I fought hard to be released. I wasn't expecting the discipline to be so harsh. I remember the shortage of men going to the floral hall(The Empire) ballroom dancing and dancing with

MORECAMBE WINGS

another WAAF. One rather ugly man found himself much in demand by hundreds of WAAFS. The only men available were officers I was blonde and very attractive and so much in demand. I was known as Blondie even to my husband. You could get a certain reputation going out with officers your friends said you were lying down for them. I know some of that did go on but I never did I was true to my husband when I married him just after the war.
TAJ: You any other memories.
Muriel D: There is a church on Sandylands which is now a block of flats, we used to go for our pay. I remember that very well going in there saluting giving your name rank and number, you got a pound a week. I remember we weren't here long enough to get close to any of the other girls. Later when I went to Bridlington to do my trade I still keep in touch with now.

BY TREVOR JORDAN

Doris T

TAJ: When did you join the WAAF ?
Doris T: in 1942 I was a volunteer I was working in an insurance office in Kendal.
TAJ: Do you have any early memories of the WAAFS?
Doris T: I was sent to Gloucester to be kitted out with uniform and then we came up to Morecambe about a week afterwards.
TAJ: Where was your billet?
Doris T: Westminster road the seventh house on the left near the school nearest the Co-op on Regent Road. There were four or five WAAFS withme but there were only two to a room. Thelady was called Mrs. Atkinson it was a private house not a hotel. I remember the beds were very hard.
TAJ: Were they provided by the RAF.
Doris T: That's right. I remember walking along the promenade with my gas mask on to go to the Central Pier for lectures and then we went to the Alhambra at the bottom end for lectures. I remember we had to catch a train from Morecambe Promenade station in the

MORECAMBE WINGS

pouring rain at 2.30 in the morning with kit bags and went to Penarth on an accounts course.
TAJ: How long were you in Morecambe.
Doris T: About a month we just paraded and had lectures. The Midland Hotel was a RAF hospital I went there once. It was a lovely place.
TAJ: For inoculations.
Doris T: No I went to the Alhambra for that, everybody queuing up.
TAJ: Any other memories of Morecambe.
Doris T: I went for dancing on the pier.
TAJ: Do you remember the footslogging?
Doris T: Oh yes I remember that but I used to enjoy marching I liked to watch trooping the colour. I always liked dancing, marching and keeping fit.
TAJ: I know you can't remember the billets but have you any wartime memories of Morecambe.
Doris T: Before I joined up I used to come with my father to the Winter Gardens for the all in wrestling.
TAJ: I didn't mean that RAF memories?

BY TREVOR JORDAN

Doris T: Well I remember if you had a stripe you were a leading aircraftwoman. When you first joined up you were an aircraftwoman 2 then you passed exams to get to your aircraftwoman 1, then leading aircraftwoman, then a corporal, sergeant, flight sergeant, warrant officer, then Flight Lieutenant but I only got Leading aircraftwoman. I remember at Gloucester you could hear the women crying wishing that they had never joined. I enjoyed the RAF I volunteered but my mother was

horrified. Unknown to me she had been to the provincial and had me deferred and I kept thinking why haven't they sent for me because I had already been to Carlisle for the medical. I went to the Labour Exchange in Carlisle and eventually I was called up. I wanted to be like everyone else I think the uniform attracted me (laughs). It was a good life I wouldn't have met my husband if I hadn't joined up. We courted four months and got engaged VE day and we got married on the anniversary war broke out 3rd of September, 1945. We were married 11 months before the birth of my son. It meant automatic discharge from the RAF.

MORECAMBE WINGS

5 FINDINGS

In the seaside resort of Morecambe the Second World War came as a surprise four days before its declaration Morecambe and Heysham Corporation announced that it would be "lights up and not black out" and BBC number one gardener Mr C.H. Middleton switched on the promenade illuminations at Happy Mount Park. The next night they were switched off and not illuminated again for another ten years. At the same time all places of entertainment were closed for the emergency (Bingham, 1990, P236).

BY TREVOR JORDAN

The hotels had been full throughout the 1939 season and they were booked up right up until October. Many had never thought that war was imminent. It came as a shock when only one guest arrived and he was told to leave as soon as possible. Loud speakers went through the streets telling visitors to leave (Interview with Kathleen G. pp40-60).

As war was declared on the 3rd of September, 1939 only one cinema was open in the whole of Britain that was on the pier at Aberystwyth. Sir Oswald Stoll in a letter to The Times questioned the wisdom of closing theatres when during First World War show business had played a vital role in maintaining the morale of civilians and servicemen. Provided they closed at ten O' clock theatres were allowed to reopen from 16th of September, 1939 (Taylor, 1992, PP17+18).

In Morecambe the advertisement in Morecambe Wings (Documents C p135-6) gives some understanding of what was available to servicemen posted here. Morecambe wings magazine's editorial stated that "we hope our column will be widely read as it is published expressly with the idea of bringing all airmen in

MORECAMBE WINGS

touch with the various activities which are thoughtfully provided for them on the station" (Cover, Document A). Though the offices were in hotels, the personnel in boarding houses and hangers in Westgate the resort was treated as an RAF station.

The airmen were divided into flights of 144 men each with one instructor per 24 men. There were 10 or 12 billets a flight which would make the average billet size 12 though the partner put the figure at 6 to 10 with 300 men here at one time for training. As the wartime population trebled to 67,000 three times the pre-war figure it is likely that this was an exaggeration (interview James R pp 87-92 & Betty F pp 25-39) remembered that the RAF allocated them 14 but you could only put one in a bed. Before the war in apartments it was not unusual for multiple bed occupancy particularly within families. Walton (1978, P123) indicated the extremes "not only did they sleep five or six to a bed but they had five or six beds to a room". By the thirties with local medical officers of health this practice was not as prevalent. Maud C stated the parents had one

BY TREVOR JORDAN

bed and the children the other with 24 guests in all. Her allocation of RAF airmen was 12 only half her pre-war capacity (pp72-80).

The RAF from its headquarters sent surveyors out to assess each apartment, guesthouse, hotel and private household to see how much room you had and whether you could take the personnel. It was your duty if you had the room you had the airmen (WAAFS after 1942, though those with evacuees were exempt (interview Mrs. K pp 81-86)

The hoteliers asked if they could take both RAF and visitors but apart from wives turning up you did one or the other for security reasons (Interviews, Betty F pp25-39, and Kathleen G pp 40-60).

Pat F (pp61-71) stated that later in the war her Mother became ill but the authorities refused her permission to be excused billeting duties and the family had to reluctantly sell their house to see it sold later at a huge profit. Pat F remembers her mother being told it was not essential war work and was still expected to do fire watching. Some nights she struggled into bed having worked an eighteen or twenty hour day looking after 15 airmen.

MORECAMBE WINGS

You couldn't refuse to billet but apparently you could hand your house over to the RAF but this then made them responsible for any damage. This way was not popular with the authorities but most landladies saw it as their duty (Interview with Pat F pp 61-71). Though Pat F's mother was not considered to be doing essential war work Maud C (pp 72-80) was the right age to be considered for female call up. She however stated that through her billeting duties as a landlady she was excused war service Winston Churchill's daughter Sarah was a WAAF billeted into West End Road. Comedian Vic Oliver had married Sarah when she was a chorus girl in C.B. Cochran's revues but being who she was didn't excuse her from war service (Taylor, 1992, PP24+25). She raised morale among the landladies by accompanying the warrant officer who paid the billeting fee every Monday. Wartime evacuee Dr. B.H. Burne who spent the period 1940 to 1945 in Morecambe remembers that "RAF and WAAFS were billeted in the boarding houses and could be seen parading and marching along the prom and square bashing behind the Winter Gardens.

BY TREVOR JORDAN

Discipline in the RAF was not harsh as in the other services as airmen and WAAFS were taught trades and their purpose was not to fight in battle. Every spare moment was spent drilling though there was bayonet and self-defence training at Middleton Towers army camp and rifle shooting on the White Lund range. The servicemen interviewed remembered the footslogging along the promenade though being young most were reasonably fit anyway. One WAAF remembered the awful blisters on her feet and being unable to take her jacket off in the hot Indian summer of 1942. One airman recalled that when they got to the Clarendon Hotel they set off into double pace but presumably only to impress the brass. The other WAAF said she quite liked the drilling but one mother insisted on watching her daughter parade much to her embarrassment. (Picture 20, P131) shows RAF airmen doing their physical training at the bandstand on the promenade.

In the L&M Newspapers special supplement (Document F, P139) to WAAF K. Watts it was a life of lectures and parades. A free comedy show was to be had by all as the girls learnt to march on the prom. March they did and passed

MORECAMBE WINGS

out next to the band stand near the nineteenth century battery (Picture 17 p128).

Apart from Pat F (pp 61-71) who stated her mother went to the Savoy café to be paid, all the rest confirmed it was practice of the RAF Warrant officers to pay billets on Monday morning (Document D, P137). Chits were provided rather than ration books for each man for the landladies to use in the shops they were registered with. Shopping took place daily as food was perishable and could only be kept in the cold cellar for a short period of time. If you had fifteen airmen that was fifteen 2 ounces of butter, fifteen 2 ounces of sugar but hoteliers had relatives in the country who could bring them poultry, dairy products and other items off the ration (Interviews Betty F pp 25-39 and Mrs K, pp 81-86). Food in Morecambe being a garrison town was plentiful there were no shortages as in other places and sometimes there was extra that could be sold onto the black market. The landlady claimed for however many personnel she was allocated with that week. There was no problem they could cook huge rice puddings, bake and make pies

BY TREVOR JORDAN

and get beast heart from the butcher which one landlady served with apple sauce and called Spruce Goose. There was ingenuity to provide large meals out of limited sources. (Interviews Betty F pp 25-39 and Kathleen G, pp 40-60).

In the trials and tribulations of the squadron commander (Document D, P137) the practice of paying billets was detailed "paying billets that Monday horror". What squadron commander would not lead his men against firmly entrenched machine guns in preference to the sullen trot from house to house. He details Lodging, Furniture, Fuel and Light allowances which is quite strange as all interview partners have said they had to manage everything out of their £1.0.6d billeting allowance including fuel and wear and tear on the billet.

Kathleen G (pp 40-60) remembers one incident where the billeting authorities told them to prepare for a contingent of airmen. After they had bought the food no one turned up and there was no apology or explanation from the RAF.

In the days before fridges food had to bought consumed within a few days. Kathleen remembers that out the Clarendon Hotel she encountered a photographer who her to smile

MORECAMBE WINGS

and snapped her (Photo 16, P127. Apparently'. reply was unprintable as can be seen by her expression, billeting authorities subjected to a mouthful from her up Kathleen and her neighbours who had appointed spokesman.

Though beds and blankets were provided by the RAF the landladies providing the sheets and the pillows. Airmen were not issued with sheets the RAF only providing these for WAAFS and officers (Taylor, 1992, P10).

James R remember an NCO inspected the billets and Airmen were told any complaints from the landladies would be put on a charge.

In the billet a senior airman was appointed to bring any problems the men may have to the NCO's so as to appease the landlady. Only Pat F (pp 61-71) remembered the senior man.

In Document B, P134, the life of the senior man is repeated. He was a sort of Lance Corporal who marched the men onto parade and dealt with problems in the billet. He also drew up a bath roster and was a go between landlady the men and RAF regiment.

The provision of bathing was a problem on average each airmen would get a bath twice a

BY TREVOR JORDAN

week but when the WAAFS came they demanded baths every day and the billeting authorities were inundated with complaints. As landladies had an automatic right of removal any complaints usually resulted in the removal of the WAAFS and their being put on a charge Hot baths were a luxury as coal was rationed and the RAF didn't provide extra funds for the RAF and WAAFS. With the airmen a bath every week was acceptable but to glamorous WAAFs it was unacceptable. The WAAFS undertaking their basic training or the nurses in the hospital were quite well liked but the office workers at the Clarendon hotel were wives of officers and could be rather difficult. Maud C invited WAAF'S as her sole guests at her 1943 wedding. See photo 21 p132 for library picture.

Newly called up boys arrived for their basic training just after Christmas in 1939. Many came from the hill farms of wales and had never seen a water closet before. One of the landladies and her mother shed tears that all these young boys would leave after their basic training not knowing if they would ever return having volunteered for aircrew (Interview with Kathleen G pp 40-60).

MORECAMBE WINGS

James R (pp 87-92) said of these boys that a lot were illiterate as probably their parents had been and the three weeks basic training was insufficient to teach them to read or write.

The Clarendon Hotel had Inspection Officers men too old to fight given high ranks within the RAF but given the task of moderating any unseemly behaviour in the billets. Morecambe Solicitor and sometime Chairman of Morecambe football club John Knape had been extremely critical of the RAF's treatment of his well healed clients the owners of the large hotels but he was remembered by those at the other end of the accommodation market for his heavy handed attitude on them and their businesses. Kathleen G (pp40-60) commented if they were old enough to fight they should be treated by the authorities as adults .

MORECAMBE WINGS

6 CONCLUSIONS

Phyllis Dixie whose nudity show at the Windmill Theatre -as tolerated by the Lord Chamberlain's office commented "we forget how young the armies were in World War Two. For many of the children who stamped their feet for more it was the first time they had seen a naked woman". Sadly for so many too, it was to be the last (Taylor, 1992, P 1 1 1).

To some the war was a Golden Age and certainly Morecambe's Ballrooms, Cinemas, and theatres were full to capacity all the year

MORECAMBE WINGS

round and in 2001 none of them now exist. Morecambe has been overtaken like many UK resorts by the cheap overseas package holiday but it still has its compensations as a resident looking over glorious Bay views.

Sixty years ago a whole generation of young people were sent to fight a fascist menace. Most landladies took to their young charges and some may even have mothered them. What is clear is that a lot didn't come back killed in action and though the billeting authorities were heavy handed most landladies saw the looking after of airmen and WAAFS as their patriotic duty. Many had relatives of their own fighting in the same war so treated their own guests as if they were honouree members of their own family.

The Golden Age is a myth it was a serious time but even in tragedy people could aspire to the highest of motives. Kathleen G took in an airmen disfigured in battle. She, Betty F's mother, Pat F's mother and Maud C and provided her charges with sometimes four meals a day.

BY TREVOR JORDAN

It was fortunate for them that Morecambe escaped serious wartime bombing. Kathleen G remembered the anti-aircraft guns used to rattle shrapnel on the roof of The Whitehall cinema (Photo 15 p127). Kathleen G may have made money even buying a horse for one of her children (Photo 14 p126). She stayed in the hotel business until 1952 long after the others ceased to do so. How she made a profit out of £1.0.6d a week when others were appalled of its derisory nature probably showed a good business brain. Ironically hostile Mrs K after the war opened her own guesthouse and remained in the business until the 1970's.

What may be nostalgia to some has to be tempered with the fact many learnt lifelong trades and skills during the war as a direct result of their war service.

Maud C, Kathleen G and Doris T met their husbands as a result of the war and Pat F became a CAA controller after training by the Royal Observer Corps in Lancaster Operations room a sort of wartime apprenticeship.

The Kensington House Visitors book (See Chapter 10) shows the fears, aspirations and hopes of a whole generation of young people. Its more than proof that the landladies treated

MORECAMBE WINGS

their guests alright and some lifelong friendships developed between them. One final point how many of those entries never came back lying in some foreign war cemetery.

When the air raids were taking place at Liverpool though it was sixty or seventy miles away the night sky was a deep red colour.

7 BIBLIOGRAPHY

Primary Sources

'Day in Life of the Senior Man' in Morecambe Wings (RAF Station Magazine)11.7. 1941 P9 in Second World War file, Morecambe Local Studies Library.

'It was a life of lectures and Parades' by K.Watts in Lancaster and Morecambe Newspapers Special Supplement 5.5.1995 in Second World War file, Morecambe Local Studies Library.

'Kensington House Visitors Book' 1-19 supplied by Pat F.

MORECAMBE WINGS

Morecambe Wings (RAF Station Magazine) 11.7. 1941 Cover in Second World War file, Morecambe Local Studies Library.
'Square Bashing Behind the Winter Gardens' in Morecambe Visitor 22.9.1976 in Second World War file, Morecambe Local Studies Library.
'Trials and Tribulations of a Squadron Commander' in Morecambe Wings (RAF Station Magazine) 6.12. 1940 P9 in Second World War file, Morecambe Local Studies Library.
'A mother to the Soldiers' Visitor 22.9.1976 as above.

Articles & Books

Bingham, Roger K (1990) **'LOST RESORT? The Flow and Ebb of Morecambe,** Milnthorpe, Cicerone Press.

Calder, Angus (1969), **'The People's War Britain 1939 - 1945,** London, Jonathan Cape.

Chant, Christopher (1989), **'The History of the RAF',** London, Regency House.

Giles, Judy (1992), 'Playing Hard to Get' working class women, sexuality and respectability in Britain, 1918— 40' in Bessell R

BY TREVOR JORDAN

(ed.) **The Oral History Project Offprints Collection,** Milton Keynes, The Open University.

Gittens, Diana (1982), 'Work Before Marriage' in Bessell R (ed.) **The Oral History Project Offprints Collection,** Milton Keynes, The Open University.

Grele, Ronald J (1991), 'Listen to their Voices', in Bessell R (ed.) **The Oral History Project Offprints Collection.**

**I am indebted to the interview partners for the photographs of the era with the exception of photo 132 of a WAAF to USAF wedding The Ladies of Bletchley Park WAAF (Women's Auxiliary Air Force) Margaret (Peggy) Mason married her USAF (US Air Force) sweetheart, James (Jimmy) Edward Stidham, in Bletchley on special licence in June 1945.
Read more: http://www.mkweb.co.uk/Celebrations/Valentines-Day/How-romance-blossomed-at-Bletchley-Park-Milton-Keynes-20140214110000.htm#ixzz35ldGIo94**

MORECAMBE WINGS

8 PHOTOGRAPHS

1. P120 T MIDLAND HOTEL
2- P120 B GROSVENOR HOTEL
3- P121 T CLARENDON HOTEL
4- P121 B BROADWAY HOTEL
5- P122 T ALHAMBRA MUSIC H
6-P122 B EMPIRE BALLROOM
7- P123 T WINTER GARDENS
8- P123 B HEADWAY HOTEL
9- P124 T RUPERRA PRIVATE HOTEL
10-P124 B VICTORIA APARTMENTS
11-.P125 T KENSINGTON GUEST HOUSE
12-P125 B HIGHFIELD APARTMENTS
13. P126 T RUPERRA 1940S VIEW
14. P126 B KATHLEEN G'S DAUGHTER
15-P127 T WHITEHALL CINEMA
16-P127 B KATHLEEN G 1940
17- P128 WAAF PASSING OUT PARADE
18- P129 AIRCRAFTMEN GROUP
19.- P130 JAMES R GROUP OF NCO's
20- .P131 DRILLING ON STONE JETTY
21.- P132 WAAF WEDDING
T- Top   B – Bottom

BY TREVOR JORDAN

1

2

MORECAMBE WINGS

3

4

BY TREVOR JORDAN

5

6

MORECAMBE WINGS

7

8

MORECAMBE WINGS

9

10

MORECAMBE WINGS

11

12

BY TREVOR JORDAN

MORECAMBE WINGS

15

16

BY TREVOR JORDAN

MORECAMBE WINGS

18

BY TREVOR JORDAN

MORECAMBE WINGS

20

BY TREVOR JORDAN

21

9. DOCUMENTS

A FRONT COVER: MORECAMBE WINGS STATION MAGAZINE
B: DAY IN THE LIFE OF THE SENIOR MAN p134
C: ACTIVITIES TO RAF IN MORECAMBE pp 135 & 136
D: TRIALS AND TRIBULATIONS TO SQUADRON COMMANDER 2. PAYING BILLETS p 137
E: SQUARE BASHING BEHIND THE WINTER GARDENS P138
F: IT WAS A LIFE OF LECTURES AND PARADES p 139
G: A MOTHER TO THE SOLDIERS p140
H: MAP OF MORECAMBE AS IT WOULD HAVE BEEN DURING WW2 p141

BY TREVOR JORDAN

A Day in the Life of a Senior Man

(All the characters in this narrative are fictitious and any resemblance they bear to any living person is purely co-incidental.)

FIVE days after joining the R.A.F., I found myself rushed into a mysterious position known as "Senior Man." My squad N.C.O. told me it was a lousy job, but having had nine months as sergeant in the Home Guard I thought it would be simple. My first big mistake. As far as I could gather I was to be a sort of Lce.-Corporal (acting unpaid).

As the majority of airmen seem to imagine a Senior Man's job is something on a par with that of W.O., Air Chief Marshal, let me spring to the defence of my fellow Senior Men by setting out the facts.

The first job in the morning is to go around and arouse the men. There are twenty men in my billet including, of course, the inevitable funny man, a chap named Onions, whose principal occupations are reclining in weird and wonderful attitudes and castigating everyone with fiendish wit.

Going down to breakfast I find Onions lying on the sofa, supporting his head in his hand with his elbow on the floor and getting up with the movement of a professional contortionist, upsets the milk all over one of the tables. Consequently I have to move quick. Start breakfast. Stop breakfast to intervene in hectic argument which looks like developing into a free fight. A.C.2 Biff asks me if I can approach Flt.-Sgt. Moses about him taking the squad. Ask why. A.C.2 Biff says that when Sgt. Moses gives orders he sounds as if he is vomiting and it makes A.C.2 Biff feel ill. Tell A.C.2 Biff that sergeants, when giving orders, are allowed to make noises resembling vomiting, a clucking hen, bellowing bulls or anything else.

Get squad outside billet—or some of them—ready to move off to parade ground. Ready to move off. Someone asks if we have to carry groundsheets because he hasn't got his. Tell him we always carry groundsheets on parade and send delinquent to fetch it. Someone else asks if we want gym shoes, because he hasn't got his. Send him for them. March squad off. Things seem fairly quiet so leg them march at ease. Jim, the Bounder, materialises from nowhere. Roars and bellows for about five minutes. Gather from his remarks I must not march squads at ease through the streets. Resolve to pray for the enlightenment of all Flt./Sgts. Hear rattle behind us as we move off and turning out to purify atmosphere.

Get in sight of Parade Ground. Observe Sgt. Sniff, with a baleful gleam in his eye, waiting and praying for me to halt squad on wrong foot. Wheel squad onto ground. See that I have brought them round too soon and will have to give them a right turn to get them nicely in position. Decide to show off and do it on the march. Unfortunately get mixed up and give left turn. Sgt. Sniff and six men go down a whirling mass of arms and legs. Thought flashes through my mind: "Can I be court-martialled for causing grievous bodily harm to an N.C.O.?" Sgt. Sniff arises with a beatific smile on his face which I discover later, was caused through knocking his head on a large stone. Effects of blow on Sgt. Sniff's head vanish and so does beatific smile. Five minutes later I gather, in between the adjectives, that (a) my squad is the worst in Morecambe, (b) I am the worst Senior Man the Service has ever had, (c) I had better go and drown myself. Two decontamination squads turn out. Resolve to pray for all sergeants.

The morning goes on with only one untoward incident. That is when we are getting ready for P.T. on the beach and one of my squad slips his trousers down and discovers he has forgotten to put on his shorts underneath, to his own mortification, the horror of three elderly maiden ladies and the huge delight of a crowd of small boys. Observe squad N.C.O. looking at me and decide it must be all my fault.

Detail arrives by runner that I am to report at Squadron Office at 1400 hours. Feverishly wrack brains to discover reason. Decide it must be a court-martial over the Sgt. Sniff affair and wonder if I can be shot. Back to billet and eat hearty lunch as it may be my last meal.

Ready to march off to afternoon parade. Observe imposing-looking personage in superfine cloth uniform approaching. Call squad to attention. Imposing-looking personage braces up. Prepare to salute and observe my mistake. Tell squad it is all right as it is only a W.O. Imposing-looking personage visibly shrinks—and so do I, five seconds later. Resolve to pray for all W.O.'s. March squad to parade ground. Told to go to Flight Office before reporting to Squadron Office. Do so. Wander about building for about ten minutes as no one seems to know where Flight Office is situated. Eventually discover door. Notices all over it. "Keep out." "Private." "No Admittance." "This goes for N.C.O.'s, too." Spend another ten minutes gingerly knocking on door. Along comes a flight-sergeant, who says: "It is no use standing there knocking, sonny, walk right in." Resolve to remove W.O.'s from list of those to be prayed for. W.O. takes me before Adjutant who also proves very helpful. Decide to remove officers from list of those to be prayed for. Remember they were not on list, so decide to bear matter in mind for future reference.

Back in the billet several of the squad ask me to demonstrate a certain drill movement. They are well aware that I can never carry it out without making a mess of it. But I must either do it and give them a laugh or earn their contempt as a funk. Someone else wants a hand to roll a gas cape. Then I have to draw up a washing-up roster and check up on baths. A.C.2 Bang asks me how he should go about becoming an N.C.O. I give him a withering look and tell him the first step is to become a Senior Man. After twenty-four hours of that he should feel that he would not become one even if the C.O. went down on his bended knee and begged him. If after that period he still feels he wants to be an N.C.O. he had better approach Sgt. Sniff when the sergeant is in his most belligerent mood. In the meantime, whilst he is waiting to become the ideal Senior Man he must learn to be a general lackey and wet-nurse, be an authority on K.R.'s and A.C.1's, acquire the wisdom of Solomon and the patience of Job, know the Royal Warrant inside out and about four thousand other things. When he does become a Senior Man he will discover his principle use in life is to provide a means for N.C.O.'s to work off their morning-after-the-night before feeling. It is a well known fact that N.C.O.'s have to work off so many "choke-offs" every day but it is not so well known that if they see they are somewhat behind in their quota the Senior Man gets the surplus.

So much for the tribulations. What of the compensations. As a Senior Man, none. I admit I am fortunately placed. I am not married; I have no ties and I am one of those peculiar people who like Service life. To me it is a *grand* change. I enjoy all of it. I am amongst a splendid crowd of fellows. And I already feel fitter than I have for years. The squad is all agreed that the N.C.O.'s of the Flight—and particularly our own N.C.O.—are great fellows. They are patient, fair and just and they know their job— a very thankless one. In short, the only blot on my landscape is being a Senior Man. Any applications for the job?

MORECAMBE WINGS

CROWN HOTEL
FORCES CAFE
FULLY LICENSED.

Skipton Street Corner
(Off Central Prom.),
(Next Door to Palladium Cinema).

H.M. Forces Only.

At *REDUCED* PRICES

Open Daily until
10-30 p.m.

CROWN CAFE
28 Albert Road

Proprietor - J. A. J. Leech.

Everything Baked on Premises.

TEA CAKES A SPECIALITY.

MORNING TEA AND COFFEE.

ROYALTY Theatre
MARKET ST., near G.P.O. Tel. 109

To-night and Saturday at 7-15.
THE PLAYERS present
WASN'T IT ODD?

Talkies. Sunday, July 13th, 7-15.
Johnny Weissmuller and
Maureen O'Sullivan in
TARZAN FINDS A SON

Monday, July 14th, at 7-15—
THE PLAYERS present
OFF THE GOLD COAST
By H. F. Maltby and Clifford Grey.

Talkies. Sunday, July 20th, 7-15.
Sonja Henie and Richard Green in
MY LUCKY STAR

TOWER
General Manager: H. R. V. Addenbrooke

Sunday, 13th July, for 7 Days—
Sunday at 7-15; Weekdays 2 and 7.

GINGER ROGERS in KITTY FOYLE
(a). Also (except Sunday) Kay Francis, James Ellison in "PLAYGIRL."

On the Stage. Friday Nights at 7-45.
STAGE TALENT COMPETITION
Open to All Members of H.M. Forces and Civilians.
Prizes: £3, £2 and £1.
Competitors must enter before the actual night.
For Entry Form and full particulars apply Tower Box Office.

DANCING EVERY EVENING
Old Tyme Night: Thursdays.

Sunday, 20th July, for 1 night only.
SPECIAL PROGRAMME OF PICTURES & GUEST ARTISTES.

Monday, 21st July, for a short season
WHAT'S GOING ON HERE?
Cast includes:
MURRAY & MOONEY
Marion Pola - Chris Joy
Dennis Lawes - 3 Calores Sisters
and other well known artistes.

NEW PLAZA
Opposite Clock Tower.
Phone 408 Phone 408

Sunday, July 13th, Four Days—
LLOYD NOLAN, LYNN BARI in
THE CHARTER PILOT
With ARLEEN WHELAN.

Thursday, Friday, Saturday—
DOUGLAS FAIRBANKS, Jr.,
RITA HAYWORTH in
ANGELS OVER BROADWAY
With THOMAS MITCHELL.

Sunday, July 20th, Four Days—
Betty Blythe, Harry Langdon,
Ralph Byrd in
MISBEHAVING HUSBANDS
Also The East Side Kids in
"HERE WE GO AGAIN."

Thursday, Friday, Saturday—
Marcia Mae Jones, Jackie Moran in
WHEN YOUTH CONSPIRES
Also "YOU'RE OUT OF LUCK."

Evenings (inc. Sundays)—Once Nightly 7-15.
Matinees Monday, Wed., and Saturday, 2-15.

ODEON
Showing at YOUR ODEON THEATRE

EUSTON ROAD - MORECAMBE
Phone 1104.

SUNDAY: 7-15 only.
MATINEE DAILY: 2-30.
EVENING Performances: 6 Continuous.

July 13th, 7 Days—
Madeleine Carroll,
Fred McMurray in
VIRGINIA
(u). Technicolour. 2-51, 6-21, 8-36.
Last Round, 8-15.

July 20th, 7 Days—
Clark Gable, Hedy Lamarr
in
COMRADE X
(u). 3-3, 6-33, 8-48. Last Round, 8-15.

July 27th, 7 Days—
Alice Faye, Don Ameche
in
THAT NIGHT IN RIO
(a). Technicolour. 3-7, 6-37, 8-44.
Last Round, 8-5.

WHITEHALL
PICTURE HOUSE, W.E. Phone 224

Sunday, July 13th, and all the week.
One of year 1941 most outstanding attractions,
ROBERT TAYLOR,
RUTH HUSSEY, WALTER PIDGEON,
Nat Pendleton and Paul Kelly in
FLIGHT COMMAND
Men of Wings take off with them in a sky-high thriller. With the mightiest Air Armada ever filmed.

Sunday, July 20th, and all the week.
The Collossus of Screen Entertainment.
Clark Gable, Spencer Tracy,
Claudette Colbert, Hedy Lamarr,
Frank Morgan and Lionel Atwill in
BOOM TOWN
The Year's Biggest Film. Takes 2 hours to show. A big, thrilling smash hit. You will never forget it.

Sunday 7-15. Weekdays, Continuous from 6-0. Second Round about 8-15. Matinees Monday, Tuesday, Wed. & Sat. at 2-15. Advance Booking Office Open Daily, 9 to 12, 2 to 4-30 and 6 to 8. We advise early booking.

BY TREVOR JORDAN

ISH ———— CHIPS

ATKINSON'S
RESTAURANT

LBERT ROAD
OPPOSITE POST OFFICE

rved inside or to carry out.

You Need Your Hair Cut —
IT WILL BE WORTH
YOUR WHILE TO FIND

ID - Gent's Hairdresser
(From Birmingham) at

VICTORIA STREET
e Minute from Central Promenade
'st left from Northumberland Street).

H.M. Forces: 6d. Quick Service.

w Do You Look in Uniform?
e Wants to Know!

MAKE SURE OF A GOOD
PORTRAIT BY A VISIT TO

AMES BLAKEY Ltd.
WEST END STUDIOS
MORECAMBE
(ext Door to Clarendon Hotel).
POPULAR PRICES.

CAFE ROY
roprietor - - R. D. Syson)
CENTRAL PROMENADE
ITERS FOR SERVICE MEN AT
SPECIAL PRICES.

GET YOUR
A F Crested Pads & Envelopes
BUTTON BRUSHES and all
CLEANING TACKLE at
ARRY'S R A F Supplies,
Lancashire Street (opp. Astoria)

SOUND INTEREST FILMS.

The programmes for Friday, 11th July and Friday, 18th July, at the Astoria Cinema, commencing at 19.00 hours, will be as follows:

Friday, 11th July, 1941.
"Daily Inspection of a Spitfire."
"Aircraft Recognition—Defiant and Blenheim IV."
"Discipline and Morale."

Friday, 18th July, 1941.
"Men of Africa."
 Britain's Administration of the Colonies.
"Britain Can Take It."
 Britain faces up to the Blitz.
"Dangerous Comment."
 Dramatic reconstructions of the disasters that can result from careless talk.
"Lessons in Aiming for Air Gunners."
"Air Firing and Tracer Method of Air Firing."
"All Hands."

STATION LIBRARY.

The Station Library has now been moved to Room 44 (Top Floor), Station Headquarters, Clarendon Hotel.

Books may be obtained on temporary loan at the following times:—

Staff and Trainees:
Sunday ... 1000 to 1200 hours.
Tuesday ... 1830 to 1930 hours.
Thursday ... 1830 to 1930 hours.
Staff only:
Saturday ... 1100 to 1215 hours.

R.A.F. MODEL AIRCRAFT CLUB.

Meetings:
Mondays—Constructional Classes at 19.00 hours in the Astoria Cinema.
Tuesdays—Constructional and Flying Classes at 19.00 hours in the Astoria Cinema.
Sundays—Flying, weather permitting, at 14.30 hours on the shore at Bolton-le-Sands, in connection with the Lancaster Aeronautical Society.
Membership: Entrance fee 1/-. Subscription 6d. per month.
Particulars from:
Mr. Horner, Civilian Ins., Bus Depot.
Mr. Johnson, C.I.; Hodgson's Garage.
Mr. Hillingsley, C.I., Bus Depot.
Sgt. Kemp, No. 7 Recruits' Centre.

Advice For Accordionists.

A/c Wm. Hubble, who is a member of the British College of Accordionists and was formerly the leading accordionist in Syd Baxter's Championship and Broadcasting Accordion Orchestra, is anxious to meet and advise any accordionists. Airmen who wish to take advantage of A/c Hubble's offer of advice should communicate with him through the Editor, Room 45, Clarendon Hotel.

MORECAMBE'S POPULAR RENDEZVOUS.

WEST END PIER
More Successful Than Ever.

Daily at 10-45, 2-45, 7-15.

FRANK A. TERRY presents

THE PLEASURE CRUISE
1941 Edition
Bigger, Brighter, Better Than Ever

LES LEE
The Popular Yorkshire Comedian.

IDA SHIRLEY
Soubrette Dancer Accordianiste.

AL. DIXON
Light Comedian, Dancer.

CHAS. WEST
Entertainer.

DORIS MARTYN
Pianist-Entertainer.

ELSIE WINNALL
The Brilliant Soprano.

ANN VERNE
Morecambe's Favourite Comedienne.

HELENA LEHMISKI'S
YOUNG LADIES
Pep and Personality—Pleasure Personified.

Fully licensed Lounge Bar
Sunshine Cafe

PIER TOLL:	H.M. Forces:
3d.	Pier Toll, 2d.
CONCERT:	H.M. Forces:
6d.	Concert, 4d.

Open Air Dancing Free

MORECAMBE WINGS

TRIALS AND TRIBULATIONS of a SQUADRON COMMANDER

2.—Paying Billets, by Job II.

"THIS moving finger writes, and having writ, moves on." With a little less verve and dash perhaps, but all the same, moves on.

The Squadron Commander, in the act of signing his 400th form 1250, looks up. The scene is the Squadron Office and the location, as the film producers say, has just been graced by the presence of a Flight Sergeant. Pursuant to the orders of his C.O., he has reported at the Squadron Office, bringing with him a recruit who sorely needs advice. Flight Sergeant announces that he is without.

Pushing away a pile of 1250's, the Squadron Commander effects a rapid change of face. After all, he has to be "all things to all men," and the transformation from blank despair to a look of fatherly wisdom is quickly accomplished. He glances to his right to make sure that his Service Bible, his inseparable Vade Necum—King's Regulations and Air Council Instructions—is in its correct place. How often had he dredged that masterpiece of English literature in search of the answer to some obscure point! How often, too, had he bent his aching brows, responding to the call of pure, enlightened scholarship, upon those pages headed "Allowances, Officers"!

Everything is present and correct. So he says, "All right, bring him in." The voice of the Flight Sergeant is heard calling upon someone or something at present unidentified out in the passage. "Attention. Quick march. Left wheel. Right wheel. Halt. Left turn. And remember to salute the officer."

The recruit, concluding these complicated manoeuvres in a gentle daze, smartly and confidently salutes the Squadron Warrant Officer. Flight Sergt. grinds his teeth, but goes on remorselessly.

"A.C.2 Witheringham-Courenay-Bentley, sir."

Flight Sergeant speaks as though he washes his hands of the whole affair. This is not one of the brightest products of his tutorial art. In fact, your mind rather dwells on the idea of a cat bringing in its mouth a small mouse and dumping same on the Squadron Office floor. But a mouse of which it is rather ashamed. Not one of its best hunting days.

"All right, Bentley, what have you come to see me about?" asks the Squadron Commander, knowing perfectly well all the time, but anxious to get something started.

"Well, sir, in a nutshell the position is this . . . ." And to emphasise his opening remarks, A.C.2 W. C. Bentley executes one or two of those expressive gestures which, in civil life, had helped to earn him fame and fortune as a salesman travelling in ladies' underwear.

"Keep your hands to your sides, can't you? Stand to attention." This from an outraged Warrant Officer.

Somewhat nonplussed at the failure of what had always been, amongst civilised business folk, an unqualified social success, the recruit gulps, looks blank for a moment, and then comes to the point without any further trimmings.

"It's about my pay, sir. I've been to see Pay Accounts and they say . . ."

But at the mention of the word " Pay Accounts," a steely look comes into the eyes of the Squadron Commander. Maybe this recruit will tell him a story which will, at long last, enable him to get a modicum of his own back on the gentlemen of the Accounts. For a long time he has been nursing a feeling of vindictiveness against a department which should be the best loved and most highly honoured in the Service. O Pay Accounts! You lovely lot of gentlemen! But to the Squadron Commander alas! the word Accounts is synonymous with a hideous duty known as "Paying Billets."

"Paying Billets!" That Monday horror! What Squadron Commander, staggering off to Accounts Office, pursued by the apologies of his Adjutant, has yet to taste the bitter cup of the remorseless duty! What Squadron Commander would not rather lead his men against strongly entrenched machine gun emplacements (given that said machine guns had all become irretrievably jammed) in preference to this sullen trot from house to house, followed by a depressed looking S.P., and trying to remember when he had last experienced such relentless rain? (It always rains on Paying Billets day. Even the Officer I/C Training reminiscences of natives disappearing in 8 feet of flood water way out at Singapore seem, momentarily, as nothing compared with this).

You pampered airmen, staggering replete from your midday dinners and wondering whether you have the courage to get more comfortable by removing your tunics in front of the windows, you have no conception of what your Squadron Commander is suffering on your behalf. You are much more concerned with the possibilities of convincing your superior officers that, much as it grieves your soul, you really must not take part in P.T. exercises in the afternoon.

Long before this the Squadron Commander, in company with a crowd of other officers who, while not being S.C.'s, are regarded as being fair game by Accounts when it comes to " Paying Billets," has said a dignified farewell to as many smirking Accounts officers as are interested, and has swung out of S.H.Q. on his grim mission, a brave smile on his lips and probably humming " If I Only Had Wings" under his breath. As part of this appeasement policy, Accounts have offered a glamour girl to join his travelling circus, but he knows that, on the principle of giving with one hand what they take away with the other, they have also probably doubled his area.

He also knows that, as he tramps from house to house, his area will steadily appear to grow longer and longer as he goes on. He wonders whether the Billeting Officer will have put troops into some billet at which no dinner has been prepared for them, or whether troops will have been taken out of a billet, at which dinner has been made ready, and, in either case, how he will smooth down a lot of ruffled feathers whilst making his get-away in as quick time and as good order as possible. He also wonders how long he can keep that intelligent look pinned on his face when queries arise.

And so remorselessly on until all the bitter dregs have been drained, and he can return to the safety of his own Squadron pen.

And in the midst of these musings I fear I have forgotten all about the problems of A.C.2 Witheringham-Courtenay-Bentley, together with the prospects of catching out Accounts. But what's the good? Has anyone ever heard of an Accounts Officer being proved wrong? Besides, what should I do about Lodging, Furniture, Fuel and Light Allowances without his kind co-operation? No. Taken by and large, he's a lovely gentleman.

Another Smashing Garrison Theatre

Fl./Sgt. SMITH SCORES AGAIN.

WE were amazed by the galaxy of talent which was presented to us at Miniature Garrison Theatre No. 3, on Tuesday, 3rd December.

To pick out individual artistes from such an excellent show is an extremely hard job, but the accompanist, A/c Addison-Smith, of B.B.C. fame, added to the success of the evening.

Garrison Theatre Swingtet was as popular as ever, and a novelty item was a London evacuee girl of 14 years of age. Tommy Seymour was among the guest artistes.—Why!!??

The show concluded with the R.A.F. Station Dance Orchestra, under the direction of S/Lt. Edgley-Fisher and conducted by F/O Rosehill, two of the dance numbers were sung by Miss Jeraldine Farrar. The show was ably compered by A/c Sherman.

TIME AND TIDE . .

Airman to Landlady: S'long, Mum. Back at 22.15.

Landlady (threatening): Look here, my lad, you'll be back at a quarter past ten and not a minute later.

BY TREVOR JORDAN

'Square bashing' behind the Winter Gardens

Visitor 22.9.76

More information about old Morecambe continues to come in by way of letters and picture following the recent publication of "The Growth of Morecambe," a pictorial history of the town published by The Visitor.

Among the latest letters is one from Dr. B. H. Burne, of Chesham Bois, Amersham, Buckinghamshire. It contains much of interest about wartime Morecambe.

Dr. Burne writes: "I was most interested to read a copy of The Growth of Morecambe on one of my periodical holiday calls into the town.

"My interest is that I spent the war years as an evacuee from early 1940 till 1945, when I went to London University from the Grammar School.

MARCHING

"The school numbers rose from about 500 to 700, under Mr. H. H. Palmer, Head, because of people like me, the children of the Civil Servants — known locally as "civvies" (National Savings, Money Order and Savings Bank), parts of the then Department of Government, the Post Office).

"My father commandeered the Grosvenor Hotel and the new buildings now hotels from the Broadway to the Grand.

"RAF and WAAFs were billetted in the boarding houses in this part of the town and could be seen parading and marching along the Prom and square bashing behind the Winter Gardens.

"There will be many airmen from the Allied Air Forces including many U.S., Poles and Czechs who remember the Midland Hotel as a Service hospital and convalescent home.

"It was still possible to have ordinary holidaymakers in the town but it was very crowded. Also, of course, there were the oil refinery and Trimpell workers.

"Anti-aircraft emplacements and pill boxes were scattered down the coast from Bare to Middleton.

"The tidal and non-tidal parts of the Bay were spiked with thousands of iron stakes to prevent enemy aircraft or gliders from landing.

"As to places of entertainment, there were nine cinemas and places of entertainment, plus the Piers.

BATTLE

"The Royalty Repertory Theatre featured the world-famous Thora Hird each week in a different role (usually an old lady), and the Winter Gardens had visits of George Formby, "We 3," Jimmy Edwards, Al Read and cultural events including the Halle Orchestra and the D'Oyly Carte Opera Company."

Also of considerable interest is part of an issue of The Visitor from Mr. Joe Maly, a secondhand furniture dealer in Morecambe.

Among items reported in the issue is a tremendous battle to get a drinks licence for the Broadway Hotel, which was then about to be built.

The hotel, which was to be a "hydro" with swimming pools, was opposed by other hoteliers in that part of the town, who considered it would rob them of trade, and an especially strong campaign was waged by the owner of the Grand Hotel — now closed, of course.

Main opponents to the granting of the drinks licence were the abstinence groups in the town and various members of the Free Churches in Morecambe. Eventually, however, the magistrates granted the licence, originally for a provisional three years.

What seems to have been the decider as far as the magistrates were concerned was that the owner told them outright that if the licence was not granted, the hotel would not be built.

The Growth of Morecambe, written and compiled by T. F. Potter, is available, price 90p, from all The Visitor shops and leading local newsagents.

MORECAMBE WINGS

It was a life of lectures and parades

IT WAS the month of July, 1942, and I was on a train bound for the WAFF training depot at Morecambe which seemed a million miles away from my home in London.

There in Morecambe, for the duration of the war, a vast transformation had taken place in a very short time. Morecambe changed from a fairyland holiday town into a mammoth training ground for women wearing the newly issued blue uniform of the Womens' Auxiliary Air Force.

The women of the WAAF arrived in their thousands and made Morecambe their home for the next few weeks or months. We learned many things never to be forgotten; for example, the correct way to march.

FIFTY years ago Mrs Kay Watts from Weymouth, Dorset, spent many weeks training with the WAAF in Morecambe.

When the war ended Kay married a man she had met on one of her postings. Her husband then joined the RAF and they travelled the world together.

Here she looks back with pleasure at her days in Morecambe.

A WAAF corporal's raucous voice meaning business could be frightening but all girls together, we pressed on regardless with heads held high.

How we tried our best to ignore the hoots of laughter from idle jokers when some poor innocent among us marched the wrong way. There on the prom the stage was set for a free comedy show for all to enjoy except we, the victims.

So life went on in dear rainy Morecambe with lectures on airforce procedure, care of uniform and equipment, the dreaded kit inspections, the much loved and long awaited pay parade and arrival of mail from home.

We emerged for the final passing out parade, miraculously transformed into shining swans gliding by on parade with not a soul out of step.

The billet I lodged in at, 9, Clark Street, was close to a church and the YMCA canteen. Also billeted with me were about eight other WAFF trainee drivers and our landlady at number 9 was a motherly kind of lady called Mrs Turner.

Four out of the eight girls were called Kathleen which caused poor Mrs Turner a great deal of frustration. We decided one of us would remain Kathleen, one re-christened Kate, one re-christened Kitty and I settled for Kay. The name Kay has remained with me after more than 50 years.

We left Morecambe when training came to an end and went our separate ways to postings far and wide. Before the war was to end many of us would serve overseas and in many strange places.

BY TREVOR JORDAN

A mother to the soldiers

World War II was an extremely busy time for Betty F▬ from Morecambe. She writes:

WHEN RAF members flooded into the town 14 people at a time were billeted at Betty's mother's guest house on Victoria Street.

They arrived in Morecambe in their hundreds and were marched through the streets until each had been signed into a guest house. There was no choice in the matter: it was a case of first come first served.

Betty, who is busy organising a reunion for people who trained in Morecambe, has vivid memories of those days: "We had to take the first 14 who arrived. Some came for six to eight weeks and others came for 16 to 18 weeks. We were paid £1 and sixpence to keep them for a week.

"I think they liked being in Morecambe. We treated a lot of them like sons. One Christmas we had more tham 14 staying and it was like one big family."

During the war everyone in Morecambe rallied together and certain buildings had very different uses: "The Midland Hotel was a hospital and the Clarendon was taken over for the RAF. Westgate was like an aerodrome and there was a huge aircraft hanger in the fields," said Betty.

Betty and her friends did a lot for the service people: "If we cleaned their buttons they gave us chocolates. I used to run a club at the British Legion and we had dancing with a band. I was a dancing teacher so I met a lot of them."

VE Day was a time of great celebration on Victoria Street: "We had a street party on VE Day. It was amazing where all the food came from."

Betty added: "I'm looking forward to meeting some of the people who stayed with us at the reunion in June. We will be taking them all over Morecambe and they will be staying at the Grosvenor Hotel."

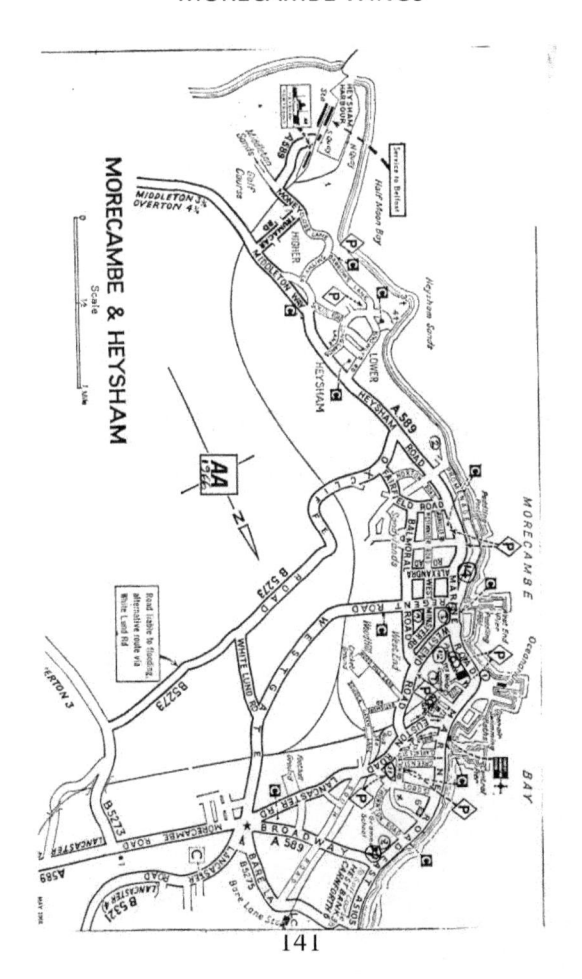

MORECAMBE WINGS

141

BY TREVOR JORDAN

10 KENSINGTON HOUSE
VISITORS BOOK

MORECAMBE WINGS

R.A.F.

1 Sandtroy Lane
Capel Newydd
Llanelly
15-4-40.

Being billeted here in 11, Kensington Rd for over 10 weeks by the Air Ministry as an airman, I rightly recommend this place to anybody, for Mrs Harper & the daughters daughters have never failed in their wonderful services. It's just like coming from home to home.

N° 971305 [A.C.1] Pritchard D.R.

BY TREVOR JORDAN

MORECAMBE WINGS

11/7/40

974828. AC2. Williams R
Mill Brook Farm.
Colne Engaine.
White Colne.
W.S.x.

For nearly 2 months I've had the pleasure of being billetted in Mr & Mrs Harpers house, and now the time has come for me to depart, and believe me its just like leaving home. I shall never forget the kindness and consideration which Mr & Mrs Harper have shown to me to me they have been more than friends.
Untill we meet again.
Bob Williams

BY TREVOR JORDAN

945664 R.A.F.V.R.
H. Jowitt A.C.1.
46 Barnsley Rd
Sandal
Wakefield
Yorks.

25/7/40.

Having being billeted at Mrs Harper's during my training in th RAF. I can fully recommend their hospitality, and I appreciate all they have done for my good-being.
Hoping we shall meet again.
H Jowitt.
My best wishes also to Mr Harper and daughters.

Miss Edna Thompson.
18 ? ? St
Dodworth
Nr Barnsley

(very satisfied.)

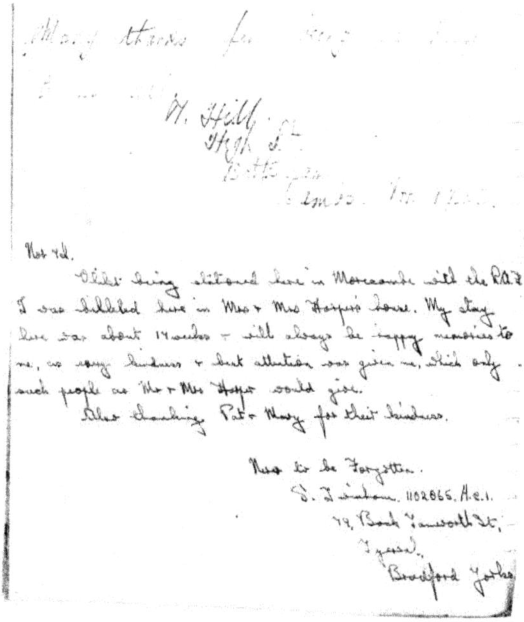

Many thanks for [illegible]

M. Hill
High St.
[illegible]

Not [illegible].

Whilst being stationed here in Morecambe with the R.A.F. I was billeted here in Mr & Mrs Harper's house. My stay here was about 14 weeks & will always be happy memories to me, as every kindness & best attention was given me, which only such people as Mr & Mrs Harper would give.

Also thanking Pat & Mary for their kindness.

Never to be Forgotten.
S. T. [illegible]. 1102865. A.C.1.
79, Back [illegible] St,
[illegible],
Bradford Yorks

BY TREVOR JORDAN

MORECAMBE WINGS

7/11/40

My stay with Mr & Mrs Harper was only three weeks far too short but those three weeks were most enjoyable & every possible attention was given to make everyone comfortable & happy & I shall never forget those days spent here. Again thanking Mr & Mrs Harper also Pat & Mary.

L.G. Barcall 1186006
1 Oak Villas
Woodfield
Ashton
Surrey

W.H. Burbidge
89 Whitworth Parade
Northampton

21·11·40.

Just a few lines to thank Mr. & Mrs Harper, for looking after me so well, during my training at Morecambe.

They have done everything possible to make me happy, and I think these are the best billets in Morecambe.

My best wishes to Mr. & Mrs Harper, Mary & Pat.

(Will meet again) Bill.

BY TREVOR JORDAN

> Dec 12. 1940.
>
> Looking through this book reminds me of quite a number of people; all endeavouring to say the same thing, that is trying to thank Mr & Mrs Hayber for the extreme kindness shown to them. To me that is an impossibility because words can't express what I would like to say. I have been billeted here for the past 19 weeks, and I have been made to feel that it is not a billet but that it is "Home" and when I find it is time to say Goodbye, it is with deep regret that I have to say it. I should also like to thank Pat and Mary for what they have done for me, and I hope that someday when we have got rid of this maniac that is trying his best to turn the world upside down that we shall all meet again.
>
> 962015 Dennis Burks
> 23 Hornely Ave
> Dodworth
> Nr Barnsley
> Yorks

MORECAMBE WINGS

112   13th March 1941.

This is the best billet one can ever have, and Mr & Mrs Harper the finest people I have come across for a long time, and I should know, as I have been about a bit. The kids, Pat and Mary, have been very nice to me. The best of Luck to all the family and I hope Pat invites me to the slaughter when she snuffles some big stiff and persuades him to keep her in luxury for life. As for Mary I hope she passes her exam O.K. and that Pat don't kick her out of bed too often. I only hope the next leading man is a model one (like me). I wish all the fellows I leave behind their L.A.C.s and I only hope they swot like I did. Thanks a lot, and I shall see you all again when this spot of bother is over, if I am not bumped off.

Pip. Pip.

Ted Read.
The Ranjon 21, Wards Road, (East)
Seven Kings
Ilford.
Essex.

BY TREVOR JORDAN

20th March, 1941

All good things come to an end,
  so we are told,
For the rich, the poor, the young and old.
And of the sweet memories, of which
  I am sure,
Are the excellent times I had at
  Kensington House.

Thanking Mr. Mrs Harper, Pat & Mary
And all the boys who made my life
  so care-free.
At the times when my life was
  almost a wreck.
When being initiated to the 'Joys'
  of being a 'Flight Mec.'

Mac.
E. J. McDermott
55, Liverpool Rd
Rudyard
Stoke-on-Trent

MORECAMBE WINGS

BY TREVOR JORDAN

28th March 1941.

Now that the time has come for my departure, I find it extremely difficult to express in words my appreciation and thanks to Mr & Mrs Harper for the kindness and consideration which they have shown for me during the sixteen weeks that I have been billeted at Kensington House, and I can only endorse the sentiments expressed by those before me. I have had a very happy time, and it is with deep regret that, all too soon, I have to say "Goodbye", but it is my sincere wish, that some day, I shall have the opportunity of returning, and I hope that next time, perhaps it will be under different circumstances, and that we shall be at peace once again.

My best wishes to Pat and Mary, I'm sure, that, whenever I think of them, I shall conjure up happy memories of my "training days" in Morecambe. The best of luck to you all.
Sincerely yours
1192301 P. Standing (Basil)
"NORTH TAYS"
11. Maxwell Road
ARUNDEL Surrey

MORECAMBE WINGS

2nd May 1941.

Nid oes gennyf lawer i ddwyd ond Diolch yn fawrhyr i Mr ac Mrs Harper am edrych ar fy ol yn arddferchog. Mi rydw i wedi mwynhau fy hyn yn rhagorol. Ac unwaith eto "Diolch" a Bendith Duw a fu arnoch chwi oll. A yda cofion a dymuniadau goreu

O'Chiwrth.

(Taffy)   Trevor Williams, Ysgolion Gerrig
Trefriw. N. Wales.

9th May 1941.   1, Upper Green, Great Bowden,
Market Harboro, Leics

I take this opportunity of thanking Mr & Mrs Harper, Pat & Mary for looking after me so well & making my stay here so happy. I sincerely hope that the day is not far distant when I can come back and talk over old times, but first we have got to wipe Hitler & his filthy gang off the face of the earth. So once more "Thank you" Mr & Mrs Harper & may the re-union with you & all the lads be sooner than we dare hope at present.   Yours sincerely
Sam Fisher

BY TREVOR JORDAN

MORECAMBE WINGS

1296546 Charles Austin
78 Campbourne Rd
Hornsey
N.8.

Thanking Mr & Mrs Harper, Pat and Mary for a wonderful time during my stay in Morecambe. Hope to return very soon.

Charles.

1072450 – T. J. Patton
18 Ardenlee Avenue,
Ravenhill Road,
Belfast N.1.

July 17th 1941.

I am extremely sorry to be leaving "Home No 2", (as 11 Kensington Road has been called by many of the boys who were visited here from time to time). I can only add my very sincere thanks to those of the many other grateful persons who have signed this book. The Harper family will always have a special place in my memory, as kindness, such as they showed me, is not easily forgotten. Yours very sincerely

Norman.

BY TREVOR JORDAN

MORECAMBE WINGS

September 1943.

As I have been so very happy it is impossible to express just how grateful I am to my second family, and I just look forward to coming down to Morecambe again during my leave. I shall be very homesick.

Marjorie Llewellin,
174 Perry Hill,
Catford, London SE6

July - September 1942.
My very grateful thanks and appreciation to my second family, for all the love and kindness showered upon me during my brief stay. Here's to seeing you once again in the happier future!

Peggy Shoult,
21, Culvers Way,
Carshalton,
Surrey

BY TREVOR JORDAN

MORECAMBE WINGS

My heartfelt thanks for the kindness that has been shewn to me here. I shall always look back on my stay at Morecambe with many happy memories, and hope to see you all once again in the future.

Brenda M. Albay,
"Lamorna,"
Shakespeare Avenue,
Langdon Hills,
Essex.

I can't thank you enough on paper for the very happy time I have had here. You have both been more than good to me and I am now looking forward to January when I hope to see you again. Thank you both for everything.

Allie W. Johnson.
2A. Ullswater Road.
Southgate. London. N.14.

It is hard to express myself on paper for all the kind things you have done for me, but here is thanking you once again, & good luck to you all.

Joan G. Costigan.
Westhays,
40, Sidney Road
Walton-on-Thames, Surrey.

BY TREVOR JORDAN

MORECAMBE WINGS

BY TREVOR JORDAN

ABOUT THE AUTHOR

MORECAMBE WINGS

Trevor Jordan has spent his life in transport having been born in 1958 and spent 20 years on the railways. Moving on railway privatization into road transport as a bus driver and most recently as a taxi driver. He lives in Morecambe the Lancashire seaside resort together with his wife Anne and two dogs a Border Terrier Snoopy and a Chocolate Labrador Rowley. Trevor studied many years to get an Open University degree and is a Lay Reader in the Free Church of England.